ARTICLE 6 OF THE PARIS AGREEMENT

DRAWING LESSONS FROM THE JOINT CREDITING MECHANISM

VERSION II

NOVEMBER 2021

ASIAN DEVELOPMENT BANK

ADB

Contents

Appendixes

Tables, Figures, and Boxes

Foreword

Tackling climate change, building climate and disaster resilience, and enhancing environmental sustainability is one of seven operational priority areas of the Asian Development Bank (ADB) under its Strategy 2030. ADB is spending a substantial portion of its own resources to support climate change mitigation and adaptation, with cumulative funding for the period 2019 to 2030 reaching $100 billion.*

Along with an increase in climate finance, reaching the objectives of the Paris Agreement demands a dramatic scale-up of private sector investments in low-carbon technologies. The Paris Agreement does not provide specific guidance on what technologies to apply in intensifying the deployment of low-carbon technologies in all sectors. However, doing so is critical to tackling this challenge.

At the 24th Conference of the Parties (COP24) in Katowice in 2018, Parties decided on a work program for the Paris Agreement Rulebook development that aims to operationalize the Paris Agreement. An important component of the Rulebook that remains to be finalized is the rules and guidelines for the international carbon markets as envisaged under Article 6 of the Paris Agreement. There was hope that the Rulebook for Article 6 would be finalized at COP26, in Glasgow in 2020. However, this important COP was postponed to November 2021 due to the coronavirus disease (COVID-19) pandemic.

Article 6 defines the framework for international carbon markets under the Paris Agreement. It provides two primary market-based options. One of the options, defined under Article 6.2, provides opportunities for countries to cooperate, bilaterally or multilaterally, resulting in the international transfer of mitigation outcomes. The countries can use these mitigation outcomes to achieve their nationally determined contribution (NDC) targets, while the host country can also benefit from an inflow of additional finance and revenue from the sale of mitigation outcomes and the diffusion of low-carbon technologies and processes.

While several countries in Asia and the Pacific have extensive experience in market-based mechanisms such as the Clean Development Mechanism (CDM) under the Kyoto Protocol, there is much less experience in the type of bilateral cooperation envisioned under Article 6.2. One notable exception is the Joint Crediting Mechanism (JCM). This pioneering project-based bilateral offset crediting mechanism has been developed and implemented by the Government of Japan to provide incentives for reducing greenhouse gas emissions through the diffusion of low-carbon technologies.

ADB has supported the development of JCM projects through the Japan Fund for the Joint Crediting Mechanism (JFJCM), which is an ADB-managed single-donor trust fund established in 2014. The fund provides grants and technical assistance to ADB-financed projects in ADB's developing member countries (DMCs) that have signed bilateral agreements with Japan for participating in the JCM. The JFJCM is part of ADB's ongoing Carbon Market Program (CMP), which has been providing technical and capacity-building support and mobilizing carbon finance for mitigation projects in ADB's DMCs since 2005.

In 2019, ADB published *Article 6 of the Paris Agreement: Drawing Lessons from the Joint Crediting Mechanism*, which describes key aspects and discusses characteristics of the JCM that enable it to be considered a forerunner for voluntary cooperation using market-based mechanisms under Article 6.2. The JCM experience

---

* Strategy 2030 Committed to mobilizing $80 billion of climate finance from own resources cumulatively from 2019 to 2030, and in October 2021, ADB increased its ambition to $100 billion during the same period.

has provided insights into how it has addressed some key elements that are likely to lie at the heart of Article 6.2 mechanisms. This publication, *Article 6 of the Paris Agreement: Drawing Lessons from the Joint Crediting Mechanism Version II*, is a sequel to the first version that describes the JCM approach to key issues: real and verified emission reductions, additional emission reductions, host-country authorization, contributions to sustainable development, avoidance of double counting, and reporting. This version also captures key lessons both for countries that have experience with the JCM and for those that are yet to participate, as they look toward operationalizing Article 6.2 of the Paris Agreement.

To demonstrate the alignment of the JCM with Article 6.2, this publication analyzed the cooperation between Japan and Indonesia under the JCM framework as a real-life example of experience from a country that has participated since 2013. In addition to assessing national-level cooperation, the publication features a specific Indonesian JCM project that is aligned with Indonesia's NDC and with ADB priorities for providing country support. It is our hope that this publication will enhance knowledge and provide important insights into how the JCM has set itself as the forerunner of Article 6.2 and the lessons learned on how future cooperative approaches can be implemented under the framework.

Bruno Carrasco
Director General concurrently Chief Compliance Officer
Sustainable Development and Climate Change Department
Asian Development Bank

Preface

The Asian Development Bank (ADB) has a long-standing engagement with carbon markets, mobilizing climate finance, and providing technical and capacity-building support for climate action in Asia and the Pacific. Under its Carbon Market 2.0, ADB will continue to mobilize carbon finance and incentivize investments in low-carbon technologies through bilateral and international carbon markets. In addition, ADB will continue to take a holistic approach to provide technical and capacity-building support to enhance developing member countries (DMCs) ability to develop and take advantage of domestic, bilateral, and international carbon markets, and, where applicable, integrated markets to scale up their efforts in achieving their nationally determined contributions (NDCs) and raising ambition over time.

As part of these efforts, ADB strives to increase knowledge and understanding of the ongoing international discussions and technical options available for the development and implementation of market-based approaches under Article 6.

Although bilateral and multilateral collaboration mechanisms under Article 6.2 of the Paris Agreement have not yet been established, there are forerunners to cooperative approaches that provide insights and lessons to learn from when considering the use of such mechanisms in the future. One such forerunner is the Joint Crediting Mechanism (JCM), which is a project-based bilateral offset crediting mechanism initiated by the Government of Japan to facilitate the diffusion of low-carbon technologies. ADB has been supporting its DMCs in engaging with the JCM through the Japan Fund for the Joint Crediting Mechanism (JFJCM) since 2014.

The ADB Knowledge Product *Article 6 of the Paris Agreement: Drawing Lessons from the Joint Crediting Mechanism* has been an important document in introducing the JCM as an example of how bilateral cooperative approaches can be designed and implemented to foster climate mitigation actions and generate mitigation outcomes. It describes the JCM experience with regard to how methodologies can be developed and authorized bilaterally, how verification can be managed jointly or bilaterally, and how mitigation outcomes can be shared among countries. It also touches upon how the JCM has anticipated several of the key elements of cooperative approaches making the need for adapting to Article 6.2 guidance proceed more smoothly.

Version II of this publication analyzes important elements envisioned in Article 6.2, namely, real and verified emission reductions, additional emission reductions, authorization, sustainable development, avoidance of double counting and reporting and implementing in real life. Furthermore, it looks at how the JCM addresses these elements and its alignment with the requirements under Article 6.2. These insights will be critical to help countries realize the relevance of the technical and institutional capacity that has been built under the JCM in enabling them to consider future modes of cooperative approaches under Article 6.2. The analysis also provides key lessons to consider in planning bilateral and multilateral approaches more broadly.

Indonesia has considerable experience in engaging with the JCM and has committed its willingness to use market-based mechanisms to achieve climate mitigation targets in its NDC. With the support of ADB's Article 6 Support Facility, Indonesia is already taking early action in the development of new market-based mechanisms under the Paris Agreement despite the delays in the adoption of the Paris Rulebook. In this version, Indonesia is presented as an example to explain the extent to which JCM implementation already aligns with the guidelines that are anticipated for Article 6.2 mechanisms and areas where further development of the mechanism is expected to be required to be considered 6.2 compliant.

This publication is intended to help climate policy makers and increase their understanding of the key implementation requirements that are anticipated for mechanisms emerging under Article 6.2, as demonstrated through a close look at the JCM. It is my hope that this publication will help all DMCs generalize and learn from JCM experience, and better understand the opportunities, potential synergies, and remaining challenges associated with developing new market-based mechanisms under Article 6.2.

Virender Kumar Duggal
Principal Climate Change Specialist
Fund Manager-Future Carbon Fund
Sustainable Development and Climate Change Department
Asian Development Bank

Acknowledgments

This knowledge product, *Article 6 of the Paris Agreement: Drawing Lessons from the Joint Crediting Mechanism (Version II)*, has been developed by the Asian Development Bank's Carbon Market Program within its Sustainable Development and Climate Change Department (SDCC).

Virender Kumar Duggal, principal climate change specialist, Climate Change and Disaster Risk Management Division, ADB, conceptualized and guided development of this knowledge product. Takeshi Miyata, climate change specialist, and Shintaro Fujii, environment and climate change specialist and fund manager of the Japan Fund for the Joint Crediting Mechanism (JFJCM), SDCC supported its development.

The knowledge product has been developed with inputs by a team of experts engaged under ADB's Carbon Market Program, which included Rastra Raj Bhandari, Takahiro Murayama, Johan Nylander, Ellen May Reynes, and Kyoko Tochikawa, whose technical inputs are greatly appreciated. Deborah Cornland and Francesse Joy Cordon-Navarro also provided their valuable inputs, which are sincerely appreciated.

This knowledge product has hugely benefited from the peer review conducted by Kentaro Takahashi of the Institute for Global Environmental Strategies, Japan, Maiko Uga of the Ministry of the Environment of Japan, and Cahyadi Yudodahono of the JCM Secretariat in Indonesia.

The timely publication of this report was made possible by the valuable coordination and administrative support of Janet Arlene R. Amponin, Anna Liza Cinco, Ken Edward Concepcion, Ketchie Molina, and Ghia V. Rabanal. Toby Miller edited the report. Prince Nicdao did the layout and composition. Edith Creus created the cover design. Jess Macasaet proofread the report and Riel Jane Tanyag handled the page proof check. Their diligent inputs are greatly acknowledged and appreciated.

Abbreviations

ADB	Asian Development Bank
AMDAL	Analisis Manajemen Dampak Lingkungan—Indonesia
BAU	business as usual
CDM	Clean Development Mechanism
CMA	Conference of the Parties serving as the meeting of the Parties to the Paris Agreement
COP	Conference of the Parties
DMC	developing member country
FVA	Framework for Various Approaches
GHG	greenhouse gas
ITMO	internationally transferred mitigation outcome
JCM	Joint Crediting Mechanism
JI	Joint Implementation
MRV	measurement, reporting, and verification
NDC	nationally determined contribution
OCC	old corrugated carton
SDIP	Sustainable Development Implementation Plan
SDIR	Sustainable Development Implementation Report
SRN	Sistem Registri Nasional Pengendalian Perubahan Iklim—Indonesia (National Registry System on Climate Change Control)
TPE	third-party entity
UKL–UPL	Usaha Pengelolaan Lingkungan–Usaha Pemantauan Lingkungan—Indonesia (Environmental Management Efforts and Environmental Monitoring Efforts)
UNFCCC	United Nations Framework Convention on Climate Change

Executive Summary

The Joint Crediting Mechanism (JCM) is a project-based offset crediting mechanism implemented between Japan and partner countries with which it has bilateral agreements that focuses on advanced low-carbon technologies and that allow the international transfer of emission reductions.

JCM was developed when a new international climate agreement was being negotiated and follows the principles of the Framework for Various Approaches (FVA) that originated from the Bali Action Plan. With the FVA being the basis for Article 6.2 of the Paris Agreement, JCM's characteristics naturally match those of Article 6.2.

This publication assesses whether the JCM is a forerunner to Article 6.2 on three levels, i.e., framework, national, and project levels. The publication analyzed the criteria, qualification, requirements, processes, and procedures using a case study project from Indonesia. Overall, the publication finds that requirements under the JCM are largely aligned with the requirements under Article 6.2, and, despite additional requirements, the experiences learned from engaging with the JCM are valuable to host countries seeking to operationalize Article 6.2. The result of the analysis will inform the next course of action to operationalize Article 6.2 through the JCM, discussing elements that need to be implemented under the JCM.

Framework Level

At the framework level, the JCM was assessed against the emerging guidance for Article 6.2 of the Paris Agreement. Article 6.2 does not provide detailed guidance on how to develop and operationalize bilateral cooperative approaches. Instead, it lays out constitution-like basic principles. The JCM has largely anticipated these principles, hence most elements are already fulfilled, although the format for presenting certain information or the nature for requiring that information may need to change, and small adjustments may be necessary to align with Article 6.2 requirements. Then there are those elements, such as corresponding adjustments, for which detailed requirements have yet to be decided by the Conference of the Parities to the Paris Agreement and therefore are not yet addressed by the JCM. These are new elements that host countries will need to consider when seeking to operationalize Article 6.2.

National Level

At the national level, Indonesia's engagement with the JCM, in terms of institutional capacity and processes in alignment with the framework, was explored. Indonesia was chosen since it is the JCM partner country with the largest track record of JCM projects. Indonesia has taken an interest in taking advance action for operationalizing Article 6.2, as highlighted in its most recent nationally determined contribution (NDC). Indonesia also has a fully functioning JCM registry in addition to its other advanced registry systems, and has also adopted its own sustainable development criteria for the purpose of JCM project approvals, providing useful insight to other countries. The analysis found that Indonesia has gained significant technical experience and expertise by participating in the JCM, which is also relevant when seeking to operationalize Article 6.2.

Project Level

A project-level analysis in relation to Article 6.2 alignment was carried out using a JCM project from Indonesia: *JCM_ID011 Reduction of Energy Consumption by Introducing an Energy-Efficient Waste Paper Processing System into a Packaging Paper Factory in Bekasi, West Java* ("the Bekasi Project"). The project was selected as it has been successfully registered and implemented and has one of the largest volumes of issued JCM credits to date. While the project was completed prior to the Paris Agreement era, it was theoretically and retroactively compared to the project procedures to Article 6.2 to draw out the lessons learned that could be transferred to meaningful action for 2021 and beyond.

Key Takeaways

Overall, of the six elements identified by the three layers of analysis, sustainable development and real and verified emission reductions were found fully aligned with Article 6.2 requirements whereas the remaining four that require action to varying degrees include additional emission reductions or "additionality", authorization, avoidance of double counting, and reporting. Regardless of these open issues, host countries can still build on their existing experiences from the JCM. As such, rather than reinventing the wheel, the key is to understand, in the national and project level circumstances, what are things that can be carried from the JCM and what are things that need additional effort to be eligible under Article 6.2.

Aim of Knowledge Product

In 2019, the Asian Development Bank (ADB) published Article 6 of the Paris Agreement: Drawing Lessons from the Joint Crediting Mechanism (Version I) which focused on introducing the JCM, its process, and available programs; and discussed key issues when considering it as a forerunner to bilateral cooperative approaches under Article 6.

Since the publication of Version I, much has happened both in the deployment of the JCM in countries and the experiences learned thereof, as well as in international climate negotiations. In particular, despite Parties not being able to agree on the "Draft Text on Matters relating to Article 6 of the Paris Agreement: Guidance on cooperative approaches referred to in Article 6, paragraph 2, of the Paris Agreement" (Draft Article 6.2 Rulebook), the last iterated proposal by the Conference of Parties (COP) Presidency provides an indication of what a final decision could look like.* Despite the impacts of the coronavirus disease (COVID-19) pandemic, there is a growing momentum to meet the goals of the Paris Agreement. This has heightened interest in international carbon markets and countries are increasingly looking to operationalize Article 6 under the Paris Agreement.

There is some level of demonstrated experience among a few countries in taking advantage of Article 6 through their engagement with pilot mitigation actions. What is often overlooked, however, is that there are more countries that are engaged with the JCM and that their experiences can also provide key insights to participating in Article 6. By looking at the current level of JCM alignment to the cooperative approaches as described under the Draft Article 6.2 Rulebook, this publication seeks to help countries build on their experiences with the JCM and explore synergies in the development of market mechanisms under Article 6. For countries that are yet to participate under the JCM, this publication will help them to understand the opportunities and challenges in doing so.

It is important to note that the Draft Article 6.2 Rulebook may not be adopted in its current form as negotiations reconvene at the COP in Glasgow. Despite the possible changes to elements that eventually get formally adopted for Article 6.2, this publication helps understand the importance of building upon the human and institutional elements developed for the JCM. In other words, it is not the primary purpose of this publication to focus on the compatibility and alignment between the JCM and Article 6.2, but rather on experience gained in the past 8 years since the inception of the JCM and accentuate on how things have evolved since the publication of Version I through implemented projects, and lessons learned that are broadly generalizable to the 6.2 mechanism.

---

* United Nations Framework Convention on Climate Change. 2019. *Proposal by the President–Draft CMA Decision on Guidance on Cooperative Approaches referred to in Article 6, Paragraph 2, of the Paris Agreement.* 15 December (third iteration).

1 Background

1.1 Article 6 of the Paris Agreement

The Paris Agreement was adopted at the 21st session of the Conference of the Parties in December 2015, superseding the Kyoto Protocol of 1997. The Paris Agreement, an international treaty ratified by 191 Parties as of September 2021, sets out a global framework to combat climate change.

At the heart of the Paris Agreement are nationally determined contributions (NDCs), which are plans and targets for national post-2020 climate actions submitted by all Parties to the United Nations Framework Convention on Climate Change (UNFCCC), setting it apart from the Kyoto Protocol that set greenhouse gas (GHG) reduction targets only for developed countries.[1]

The implication for this expansion of countries taking on emission reduction or policy targets is far-reaching not only for the broadening of the effort against climate change, but also in the context of international carbon markets. For the first time, formal demand for mitigation outcomes will exist in developing countries, leading to an important distinction between the Kyoto Protocol and Paris Agreement—the need to formally account for mitigation outcomes on both sides rather than only the acquiring side when such outcomes are transferred internationally.

Article 6 of the Paris Agreement, which deals with voluntary international cooperation for Parties to implement their NDCs, and more specifically Article 6.2, is a product of this changing landscape.

Article 6.2 stipulates that countries may cooperate voluntarily in a decentralized manner, i.e. bilaterally (or multilaterally), to achieve and transfer mitigation outcomes, provided certain criteria such as avoidance of double counting are met.[2] UNFCCC oversight is likely to be limited to specific functions such as reporting for the purpose of transparency. Parallels may be drawn with the JCM, a bilateral mechanism, as well as transborder linkages of emissions trading schemes. The detailed process for internationally transferred mitigation outcomes (ITMOs) has not yet been operationalized.

Development of bilateral/multilateral approaches under Article 6.2 that operate in alignment with the Paris Agreement principles, but with few UNFCCC regulations, i.e., operationalization of Article 6.2, have started. There are three main factors influencing such development. One, a bilateral/multilateral approach allows development of mechanisms based on agreement among the involved parties without the need for obtaining international consensus. Two, the history of negotiations around FVAs shows that countries were considering alternatives to the CDM from as early as 2007, however the Conference of Parties (COP) could not reach an agreement. In the meantime, the JCM started its implementation in 2013. Finally, the considerable autonomy promised to individual Parties under Article 6.2 allowed countries to start implementing new approaches even before the Article 6 rulebook is finalized. In fact, numerous entities are already initiating such actions and implementing pilot activities under Article 6.2. Examples are summarized below (Table 1).

---

[1] In terms of compliance, the achievement of emission reduction plans and targets as stated in the NDC under the Paris Agreement is not legally binding, although the submission of the NDC is. Under the Kyoto Protocol, industrialized countries took on legally binding emission reduction commitments; D. Bodansky. 2016. The Legal Character of the Paris Agreement. *Review of European, Comparative, and International Environmental Law*, forthcoming. 22 March.

[2] The term "countries," as used in this paper, has the same meaning as "Parties" to the Paris Agreement.

Table 1: Examples of Article 6.2 Mechanism Pilot Activities

Entities	Types of Pilot Activities Thus Far
Foundation for Climate Protection and Carbon Offset (KliK)[a]	Domestic biogas Waste management Solar photovoltaics, solar lanterns, solar home systems Improved cooking system Small and medium enterprise industry Energy efficiency
Climate Cent Foundation (CCF)[b]	Electric vehicles Domestic biogas Solar photovoltaics, solar lanterns, solar home systems Improved cooking system
Swedish Energy Agency (SEA)[c]	Energy efficiency households Biogas Solar photovoltaics Renewable mini grids Geothermal energy Firm renewable energy Ground source heat pumps Reducing high global warming potential hydrofluorocarbons for cooling Biogas waste banks Industrial waste Rural solar
Carbon Initiative for Development (Ci-Dev)[d]	Clean and improved cooking Rural electrification Biodigestors Kenya small hydro program of activities Kenya solar lighting program Clean cookstove initiative Ethanol cookstoves Biogas Off-grid renewable energy Rural electrification
Global Green Growth Institute (GGGI)[e]	Energy Agriculture Green cities
Transformative Carbon Asset Facility (TCAF)[f]	Renewable energy programs Waste sector program City-level program Island states program

[a] More information is available at Foundation for Climate Protection and Carbon Offset (KliK). Program.
[b] More information is available at Climate Cent Foundation. Pilot Activities under the Paris Agreement.
[c] More information is available at Swedish Energy Agency.
[d] More information is available at Carbon Initiative for Development (Ci-Dev). About.
[e] More information is available at Global Green Growth Institute (GGGI). Swedish Energy Agency and Global Green Growth Institute Partner to Establish Article 6 Activities; GGGI. Media Advisory: Designing Policy Approaches Under Article 6.
[f] More information is available at Transformative Carbon Asset Facility. Approach.

Source: UNEP DTU Partnership. Centre on Energy, Climate and Sustainable Development. UNEP DTU Article 6 Pipeline Analysis and Database (accessed 19 September 2021).

The cooperative approach, which shows much promise to help countries use market mechanisms to achieve their NDCs and raise ambition over time, enables governments and stakeholders to hammer out agreements that more carefully and flexibly take into account national circumstances and their priorities.

Together with the concrete actions mentioned above, this expectation is perhaps best exemplified by the recent analysis by the UNFCCC Secretariat that a far greater number of countries have expressed explicit indication of their intention to use the Article 6.2 cooperative approach to meet part of their NDC targets than those that have expressed similar intention to use the Article 6.4 centralized approach.[3]

1.2   The Joint Crediting Mechanism

The Joint Crediting Mechanism (JCM) is a project-based offset crediting mechanism implemented between Japan and 17 partner countries through bilateral agreements that allows the international transfer of emission reductions.

The JCM aims to facilitate the mitigation of GHG emissions through diffusion of leading low-carbon technologies, products, systems, services, and infrastructure. The GHG emission reductions or removals achieved through the JCM projects are primarily intended to be used by Japan and the partner countries to achieve their respective targets specified in the respective NDCs under the Paris Agreement (Figure 1).

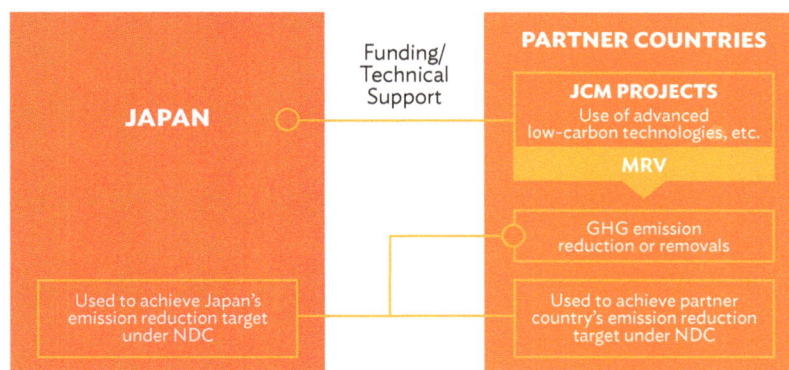

Figure 1: Overview of the Joint Crediting Mechanism

GHG = greenhouse gas; JCM = Joint Crediting Mechanism; MRV = measurement, reporting, and verification; NDC = nationally determined contribution.
Source: Government of Japan. 2021. *Recent Developments of the Joint Crediting Mechanism (JCM)*. July.

While the JCM provides several types of support, typically, a JCM project involves funding and technical support from Japan to implement advanced low-carbon technologies in the partner country. The real and verified GHG emission reductions, issued as JCM credits, are then shared between the governments of Japan and the partner country and respective project participants to achieve both countries' emission reduction targets.

The JCM aimed to be more flexible in the approach throughout the project cycle process and regarding key elements including demonstrating additionality and ensuring overall reduction in global GHGs, as further discussed in the section 2.1.3.

---

[3]   Conference of the Parties Serving as the Meeting of the Parties to the Paris Agreement. 2021. *Nationally Determined Contributions under the Paris Agreement–Synthesis Report by the Secretariat*, FCCC/PA/CMA/2021/2. 26 February.

1.3   Supporting Programs for the Joint Crediting Mechanism

There are three major financial support programs to implement JCM projects.[4] These are the JCM Financing Program for Model Projects, JCM Demonstration Projects, and Japan Fund for the Joint Crediting Mechanism.

(a)   JCM Financing Program for Model Projects

The Ministry of the Environment, Japan (MOEJ) implements the JCM Financing Program for Model Projects to promote the implementation of mitigation projects. MOEJ finances up to 50% of the initial cost of a project in developing countries that utilizes leading low-carbon or decarbonizing technologies. For those that do so through leasing business, MOEJ finances 10% of the total leasing charge, including interest. Project participants are required to conduct measurement, reporting, and verification (MRV) of GHG emission reductions. The verified and issued emission reductions (i.e., JCM credits) will then be shared between Japan and the JCM partner country to achieve their respective emissions reduction goals. There are 194 projects being developed in the partner countries as of September 2021. They belong to the sectors of energy efficiency, renewable energy, effective use of energy, transport, and/or waste to energy.

(b)   JCM Demonstration Projects

JCM Demonstration Projects are implemented by New Energy and Industrial Technology Development Organization to demonstrate the effectiveness of advanced low-carbon technologies in the partner countries and the associated MRV. Under this scheme, there are 11 projects as of February 2021. The projects introduce advanced technologies for energy efficiency improvement and renewable energy.

(c)   Japan Fund for the Joint Crediting Mechanism (JFJCM)

JFJCM is a trust fund administered by ADB, established in 2014 with contribution by the Government of Japan. The fund has been encouraging the adoption of advanced low-carbon technologies in ADB-financed and administered projects utilizing the JCM. JFJCM provides grants and technical assistance to sovereign and nonsovereign projects in ADB DMCs that have signed bilateral agreements with the Government of Japan (Figure 2).

The JFJCM is expected to contribute to sustainable development and support the efforts of DMCs to implement their NDCs under the Paris Agreement. A list of all JFJCM projects is provided in Appendix 1.

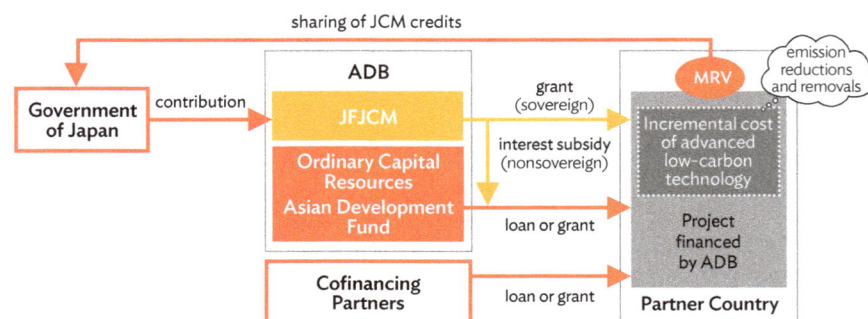

Figure 2: How the Japan Fund for the Joint Crediting Mechanism Provides Support

ADB = Asian Development Bank; JCM = Joint Crediting Mechanism; JFJCM = Japan Fund for the Joint Crediting Mechanism; MRV = measurement, reporting, and verification.
Source: Development Asia. Advanced Battery Technology to Integrate Intermittent Renewables in the Maldives.

---

[4]   Outside of the three major financial support programs, there are some others, such as those for the Reducing Emissions from Deforestation and Forest Degradation in Developing Countries (REDD+) and for fluorinated gases.

Box 1: Japan Fund for the Joint Crediting Mechanism Support for Preparing Outer Islands for Sustainable Energy Development Project

Maldives has begun gearing up for large-scale renewable energy production, with a project named Preparing Outer Islands for Sustainable Energy Development (POISED). The POISED project started in 2015 and has installed solar photovoltaic–battery–diesel hybrid systems in over 70 outer islands, including grid upgrades, energy management systems, and Supervisory Control and Data Acquisition systems to monitor the outer islands' power system from Malé. To date, POISED has helped install more than 10.5 megawatts (MW) of solar photovoltaic and 5.6 megawatt-hours (MWh) of battery storage in Maldives' outer islands.

In the island of Addu, the second-largest inhabited island in the country, POISED initially introduced 1.6 MW of solar photovoltaic power. Subsequently, with a $5 million grant from the Japan Fund for the Joint Crediting Mechanism, the project introduced an advanced lithium-ion battery energy storage system (BESS) with 0.5 MWh capacity with high-speed charge and discharge features, and an energy management system.

The project completed commissioning in August 2021 and has started operations. With the advanced BESS and energy management system, also commonly known as a "smart grid," the fluctuation of the variable solar photovoltaic power generation can be smoothed out, contributing to increasing solar photovoltaic penetration capacity (33% to 54%), increasing grid stability, and optimizing the operation of diesel generators. The intervention also reduces the cost of electricity supply and allows more renewable energy integration in the future, including private sector investment in solar energy on Addu. The expected emission reduction of this project is approximately 1,300 tons carbon dioxide equivalent (tCO_2e) per year based on the approved Joint Crediting Mechanism (JCM) methodology MV_AM002. A project design document to register this project as a JCM project is under development, and the first issuance of JCM credits is expected in 2022.

The project will bring environmental, social, and economic co-benefits to contribute to the Sustainable Development Goals, such as improved energy security and trade balance of Maldives due to reduction of imported diesel oil use as the country heavily depends on it for power generation; improved local air quality; and increased income-generating opportunities and skilled labor.

Small island countries like Maldives can replicate the introduction of these advanced low-carbon technologies to increase renewable energy penetration for achieving decarbonization while ensuring sustainable development.

BESS at the project site and EMS in the control room (Photo credit: ADB).

Source: Asian Development Bank.

1.4 Joint Crediting Mechanism Achievements

At the time of its launch in 2013, the JCM had seven partner countries along with the Government of Japan. As of October 2021, 17 countries have bilateral agreements with the Government of Japan, with 68 registered projects (Table 2).

Table 2: Progress of the Joint Crediting Mechanism in Partner Countries
(as of October 2021)

Partner Country	Start from	Number of Registered Projects	Number of Approved Methodologies	Pipeline (JCM Financing Program and Demonstration Projects in FY 2013–2021)
Mongolia	Jan 2013	5	3	9
Bangladesh	Mar 2013	3	3	5
Ethiopia	May 2013	–	3	1
Kenya	Jun 2013	2	3	3
Maldives	Jun 2013	1	2	3
Viet Nam	Jul 2013	14	15	40
Lao PDR	Aug 2013	1	3	7
Indonesia	Aug 2013	23	28	46
Costa Rica	Dec 2013	1	3	2
Palau	Apr 2014	4	1	5
Cambodia	Apr 2014	2	5	6
Mexico	Jul 2014	–	1	6
Saudi Arabia	May 2015	1	1	2
Chile	May 2015	1	2	8
Myanmar[a]	Sep 2015	1	5	9
Thailand	Nov 2015	9	15	48
Philippines	Jan 2017	–	2	16
Total	**17**	**68**	**95**	**216**

FY = fiscal year, JCM = Joint Crediting Mechanism, Lao PDR = Lao People's Democratic Republic.
[a] Information provided on Myanmar is as of 31 December 2020.
Source: Government of Japan. 2021. *Recent Developments of the Joint Crediting Mechanism (JCM)*. July; Joint Crediting Mechanism; Joint Crediting Mechanism. 2021. Preliminary Selection Result for Financing Program for JCM Model Projects in FY2021 (2nd Selection). 27 September.

Over these years, several experiences have been learned from the engagement with the JCM, including the need for technical and policy capacity-building support to infrastructural needs such as those required for robust accounting needed in host countries to operationalize any type of bilateral market mechanism.

Being the only deployed cooperative mechanism for several years, the JCM has been able to test in real-life situations with real projects, and fine-tune its approach to bilateral cooperation throughout the project cycle, including sustainable development criteria and setting of reference emission levels reflecting partner country circumstances.

Among notable achievements is the setting up of the JCM registries in partner countries that ensures no double counting. In countries such as Indonesia, the head start the JCM has had means that its registry is already connected to the national registry, making it just short of complete alignment with Article 6.2. and credits have been issued and distributed to each of the partner countries and Japan.

Based on these achievements and the promise the JCM shows to be a full-fledged Article 6.2 mechanism, the Government of Japan has extended the JCM to at least 2030 with the view to coinciding with the implementation period of the Paris Agreement.

2 The Cooperative Approach

Article 6.2 does not provide detailed guidance on how to develop and operationalize bilateral cooperative approaches. Instead, it lays out constitution-like basic principles. Crucially, it does not dictate a particular form of cooperative mechanism(s). Provided certain conditions are met, the Parties are free to agree to a mechanism(s) among themselves.

In relation to actual operationalization, there is a need to finalize the Paris Agreement Rulebook, which will contain operational guidance under Article 6.2. While the Rulebook is yet to be finalized, some progress has been made in the development of Article 6.2 guidance since the publication of Version I of this knowledge product. At the time of the publication of Version I, many elements of Article 6.2 were still unclear, and negotiators were considering a large number of options and approaches. However, at COP25 held in December 2019 in Madrid, the "Draft Text on Matters relating to Article 6 of the Paris Agreement: Guidance on cooperative approaches referred to in Article 6, paragraph 2, of the Paris Agreement" (Draft A6.2 Rulebook) was prepared with narrowed-down options and additional details on many of the key elements, which serve as the basis for the analysis and discussion in this publication.[5]

When the Draft A6.2 Rulebook is broken down, there are six essential requirements. These are explained in the chronological order as they relate to the project development cycle, rather than in the order they appear in the Draft A6.2 Rulebook.[6]

(i)   Real and verified emission reductions
(ii)   Additional emission reductions
(iii)   Authorization
(iv)   Sustainable development
(v)   Avoidance of double counting
(vi)   Reporting

Each of these are discussed in detail in the ensuing sections.

2.1 Real and Verified Emission Reductions

Similar to the requirements for Clean Development Mechanism/Joint Implication (CDM/JI) credits under the Kyoto Protocol,[7] there is a specific requirement that ITMOs need to be "real" and "verified."

Ensuring high environmental integrity of ITMOs requires a robust approach to quantifying, and third-party *ex post* verification of the emission reductions.

---

[5] United Nations Framework Convention on Climate Change. 2019. *Proposal by the President–Draft CMA Decision on Guidance on Cooperative Approaches referred to in Article 6, Paragraph 2, of the Paris Agreement.* 15 December (third iteration).

[6] In this publication, any reference to the requirements of Article 6.2 refers to the requirements listed under the Draft A6.2 Rulebook.

[7] Comparison and references to the requirements under the Clean Development Mechanism (CDM) in this publication are made solely for information purposes, as many countries are familiar with the CDM processes and requirements.

Box 2: Qualities of Internationally Transferred Mitigation Outcomes According to the Draft Article 6.2 Rulebook

1. Internationally transferred mitigation outcomes (ITMOs) from a cooperative approach are:

    (a) Real, verified, and additional;

    (b) Emission reductions and removals, including mitigation co-benefits resulting from adaptation actions and/or economic diversification plans, or the means to achieve them, when internationally transferred;

    (c) Measured in metric tons of carbon dioxide equivalent (tCO_2e) in accordance with the methodologies and metrics assessed by the IPCC and adopted by the Conference of the Parties serving as the meeting of the Parties to the Paris Agreement or in other non-greenhouse gas (GHG metrics) determined by participating Parties that are consistent with the nationally determined contributions (NDCs) of the participating Parties;

    (d) From a cooperative approach referred to in Article 6, paragraph 2 of the Paris Agreement, (hereinafter referred to as a cooperative approach) that involves the international transfer of mitigation outcomes authorized for use towards an NDC pursuant to Article 6, paragraph 3 of the Paris Agreement;

    (e) Generated in respect of or representing mitigation from 2021 onwards;

    (f) Mitigation outcomes authorized by a participating Party for use for international mitigation purposes other than achievement of its NDC or for other purposes, including as determined by the first transferring participating Party (hereinafter referred to as other international mitigation purposes);

    (g) 6.4 ERs under the mechanism established by Article 6, paragraph 4 when they are internationally transferred. (emphasis supplied)

Source: United Nations Framework Convention on Climate Change Secretariat. Draft Text on Matters relating to Article 6 of the Paris Agreement: Guidance on Cooperative Approaches Referred to in Article 6, Paragraph 2, of the Paris Agreement. Version 3. 15 December 2019.

The basic steps toward verified emission reductions involve third-party checks on input values, the implementation status of the action contributing to the emission reduction, and monitored real-life data of the implemented action (Figure 3). Under the CDM, validation occurs prior to project implementation, followed by verification(s) after project implementation.[8] Others allow the validation and first verification to be carried out either separately or together.

Emission reductions are presently calculated in multiple ways, depending on factors such as the market (compliance or voluntary), and their intended end use (claiming a mitigation effort or for promotional purposes such as labelling).

Although discussions as to how stringent these quantification and verification methods should be are still ongoing, given the language of the Draft Article 6.2 Rulebook for ITMOs to be real and verified, mechanisms will clearly need to adopt higher standards for quantification and verification similar to existing compliance-purpose mechanisms such as the CDM.

---

[8] An exception to this general rule applies to component project activities within programs of activities.

Figure 3: Verified Emission Reductions

Pre-implementation

PROJECT PLANS
- Installed capacity
- Expected operating hours
- Start up fuel usage

BASELINE CIRCUMSTANCES
- Grid connected or captive
- Base load or peak load
- Operating margin or build margin

Baseline Emission - Project Emission = **Emission Reduction ESTIMATION**

Post-implementation

IMPLEMENTATION PROJECT
- Actual installed capacity
- Actual operating hours
- Actual start up fuel usage

Baseline Emission - Project Emission = **VERIFIED Emission Reduction**

Source: Asian Development Bank.

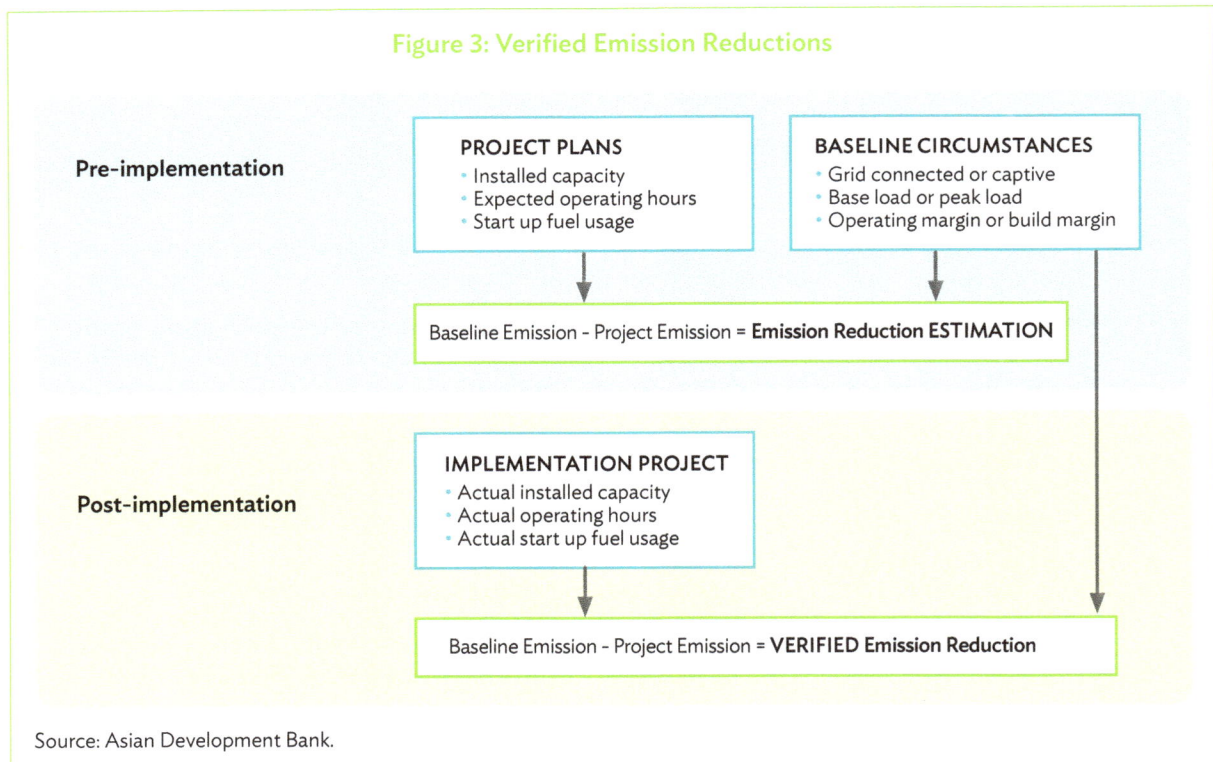

2.2   Additional Emission Reductions

The Draft Article 6.2 Rulebook also stipulates that emission reductions be "additional" in addition to being real and verified. See Box 3.

A project's emission reductions are additional if those represent reductions from the baseline emission level, where the baseline is the most likely counterfactual scenario that would have occurred in the absence of that project. For example, if a 20-year-old air conditioning unit showed signs of malfunctioning and was replaced by a new off-the-shelf model that used half the energy, there is an immediate emission reduction of 50%. But despite the emission reduction being real, it is a business-as-usual (BAU) course of action and not additional.

There is no doubt that ITMOs must represent additional emission reductions to ensure the environmental integrity of the Paris Agreement. This is particularly relevant in the present context as all Parties to the Paris Agreement have reduction targets and will have little interest in allowing non-additional emission reductions to leave its borders. However, there is ongoing debate as to how to establish additional emission reductions.

There are currently three notable examples of methods to establish "additionality":

Investment analysis: An approach centering on assessing the investment choices of project owners, additionality exists for a project where it can be established that it does not represent the most financially attractive course of action. This is one of two methods adopted by the CDM.

Positive listing: An approach centering on assessing the promulgation of advanced technologies. Additionality exists for a positive list of technologies, typically representing technologies not yet common in a particular country or industry within that country. This is also adopted by the CDM in limited circumstances.

Reference emissions setting: An approach where the most likely baseline emission level/trajectory is estimated, and where additionality is deemed to exist where the emission from a project is less than that reference level. This is the method adopted by the JCM.

Each of these methods has advantages and disadvantages, as well as criticisms.

It is noted that additionality is a concept that is applicable to a baseline-and-crediting mechanism, which both the CDM and the JCM are. It is reiterated that under the Paris Agreement, all countries have taken on targets for climate change action. When all countries have ambitious targets in the respective NDCs and are fully and appropriately accounting for their GHG emissions and tracking ITMOs, additionality and ambition become synonymous, and there will be no need to prove additionality at a project level.[9] However, we are far from this point, and the concept of additional emission reductions will remain highly relevant for 6.2 mechanisms.

At this nascent stage of the Paris Agreement era, it is expected that alignment of the reference emission level to a Party's NDC target will be attempted on a case-by-case basis, discussed, and agreed upon bilaterally.

2.3 Authorization

Box 3: Paris Agreement Article 6.3

The use of internationally transferred mitigation outcomes to achieve nationally determined contributions under this Agreement shall be voluntary and authorized by participating Parties.

Source: *Paris Agreement*, Paris, 12 December 2015, *United Nations Treaty Series*, No. 54113.

The use of ITMOs under the Article 6.2 approach requires formal authorization by the participating Parties, as stipulated in Article 6.3.[10]

There are two aspects to the discussion on authorization. The first is procedural. The second is its nature.

For the procedural aspect, while authorization is clearly a prerequisite, the specific mode of authorization is not outlined in the Draft Article 6.2 Rulebook. Given the decentralized nature of the Article 6.2 approach, it is expected that there will be significant flexibility as to the **mode of authorization**. For example, it is likely that bilateral (or joint) authorizations by the host and acquiring countries, and unilateral authorizations by each of the host and acquiring countries similar to the approvals under the CDM, will both be acceptable. It is noted that authorization and approval by governments are often used interchangeably. In this paper, the term "authorization" is used to refer specifically to Article 6.2 authorizations for ITMOs, an action which is newly

---

[9] A. Michaelowa et al. 2019. Additionality Revisited: Guarding the Integrity of Market Mechanisms under the Paris Agreement. *Climate Policy*. 19 (10). pp. 1211–1224. The authors argue that that the possibility of generating "hot air" under nationally determined contributions (NDCs) requires an independent check of the NDC's ambition. If the NDC of the transferring country does contain "hot air," or if the transferred emission reductions are not covered by the NDC, a dedicated additionality test should be required.

[10] Such authorization also considers sustainable development and avoidance of double counting, which are further explained separately in Sections 2.1.1 and 2.1.5.

necessitated under the Paris Agreement. Other types of affirmative decisions by governments are deliberately termed "approval."

On the **nature of authorization**, some caution needs to be exercised to understand that the nature of authorization by countries, particularly for the country acting as host to the mitigation activities, will be different under the Paris Agreement as compared to under the Kyoto Protocol. Under the Kyoto Protocol, as host countries had no emission reduction commitments, the approval of CDM activities only entailed a confirmation of voluntary participation and contribution to sustainable development.

Under the Paris Agreement, where all countries have commitments as stipulated in their NDCs, in addition to the confirmations of voluntary participation and contribution to sustainable development, the host country would naturally need to ensure that its compliance to its NDC is not unduly compromised by authorizing ITMOs from an Article 6.2 activity.

Being a voluntary measure, the conditions for authorization will be determined by each participating country.

2.4 Sustainable Development

Box 4: Paris Agreement Article 6.2

Parties shall, where engaging on a voluntary basis in cooperative approaches that involve the use of internationally transferred mitigation outcomes towards nationally determined contributions, promote sustainable development and ensure environmental integrity and transparency, including in governance, and shall apply robust accounting to ensure, inter alia, the avoidance of double counting, consistent with guidance adopted by the Conference of the Parties serving as the meeting of the Parties to this Agreement.

Source: *Paris Agreement*, Paris, 12 December 2015, *United Nations Treaty Series*, No. 54113.

Promotion of sustainable development is a key requirement of Article 6.2 and is specifically mentioned in the Paris Agreement itself.

ADB's DMCs prioritized SDG targets and will be setting their nationally determined sustainable development priorities under Article 6. It is of particular importance that a definition of sustainable development is not imposed on DMCs but rather is decided by them, and therefore the Article 6.2 mechanisms must assess sustainable development specifically from the viewpoint of alignment to the host country's national SDG targets and implementation plans. This is consistent with the Draft Article 6.2 Rulebook that also states each participating Party include in its biennial transparency reports information on how each cooperative approach in which it participates is "consistent with the sustainable development objectives of the host Party, noting national prerogatives."

2.5 Avoidance of Double Counting

Box 5: Draft Article 6.2 Rulebook Annex Item III B.8

Each participating Party shall apply corresponding adjustments in a manner that ensures: transparency, accuracy, completeness, comparability and consistency; that participation in cooperative approaches does not lead to a net increase in emissions within and between NDC implementation periods; that corresponding adjustments shall be representative and consistent with the participating Party's NDC implementation and achievement.

Source: United Nations Framework Convention on Climate Change Secretariat. Draft Text on Matters relating to Article 6 of the Paris Agreement: Guidance on Cooperative Approaches Referred to in Article 6, Paragraph 2, of the Paris Agreement. Version 3. 15 December 2019.

Avoidance of double counting for ITMOs is paramount for environmental integrity and ensuring that a net increase in global emissions does not occur.[11] There are several types of double counting that can occur: double issuance, double claiming, double use, and double purpose.

The transition from the Kyoto Protocol to the Paris Agreement and the new need for all countries to formally account for their emissions brings to the forefront concerns regarding "double claiming," which occurs if the same emission reductions are accounted more than once toward attaining mitigation pledges, both by the country where the reductions occur, through the reporting of its reduced GHG emissions, and by the country using the issued unit.[12]

Corresponding adjustments are the main tool that will be used to avoid double counting/double claiming of emission reductions from Article 6 activities. A corresponding adjustment is where the ITMOs, once "first transferred" and counted as part of the acquiring country's NDC achievement, are discounted from the host country's NDC achievement so that the mitigation outcome is not double counted (Figure 4). A corresponding adjustment only occurs at first transfer for the host country. Even if the acquiring country then decides to further transfer those ITMOs to a third country, this does not affect the host country whose NDC achievement has already been adjusted.

ITMOs are to be measured in accordance with the methodologies and metrics assessed by the Intergovernmental Panel on Climate Change and adopted by the Conference of the Parties serving as the meeting of the Parties to the Paris Agreement (CMA) or in other metrics determined by participating countries that are consistent with the NDCs.[13]

---

[11] The Paris Agreement has a provision for the Article 6.4 mechanism related to overall mitigation of global emissions in one of its articles (Article 6.4 (d)). However, it does not have a similar provision on cooperative approaches. Ongoing negotiations and the Draft A6.2 Rulebook text indicate that this may be voluntary, and as such encouraged, but not an obligation. Objections to introducing overall mitigation of global emissions for Article 6.2 comes both from the formal side (not a provision of Article 6) and the practical (if this is required when linking to emissions trading systems, how should be done?). See ADB. 2020. *Decoding Article 6 of the Paris Agreement Version II*. Manila.

[12] L. Schneider, A. Kollmuss, and M. Lazarus. 2014. Addressing the Risk of Double Counting Emission Reductions under the UNFCCC. Stockholm Environment Institute Working Papers. No. 2014-02. Stockholm: Stockholm Environment Institute.

[13] Both Japan and Indonesia have adopted as their metric the Global Warming Potentials of a 100-year time horizon as presented in the Intergovernmental Panel on Climate Change Fourth Assessment Report. UNFCCC. Global Warming Potentials (IPCC Fourth Assessment Report).

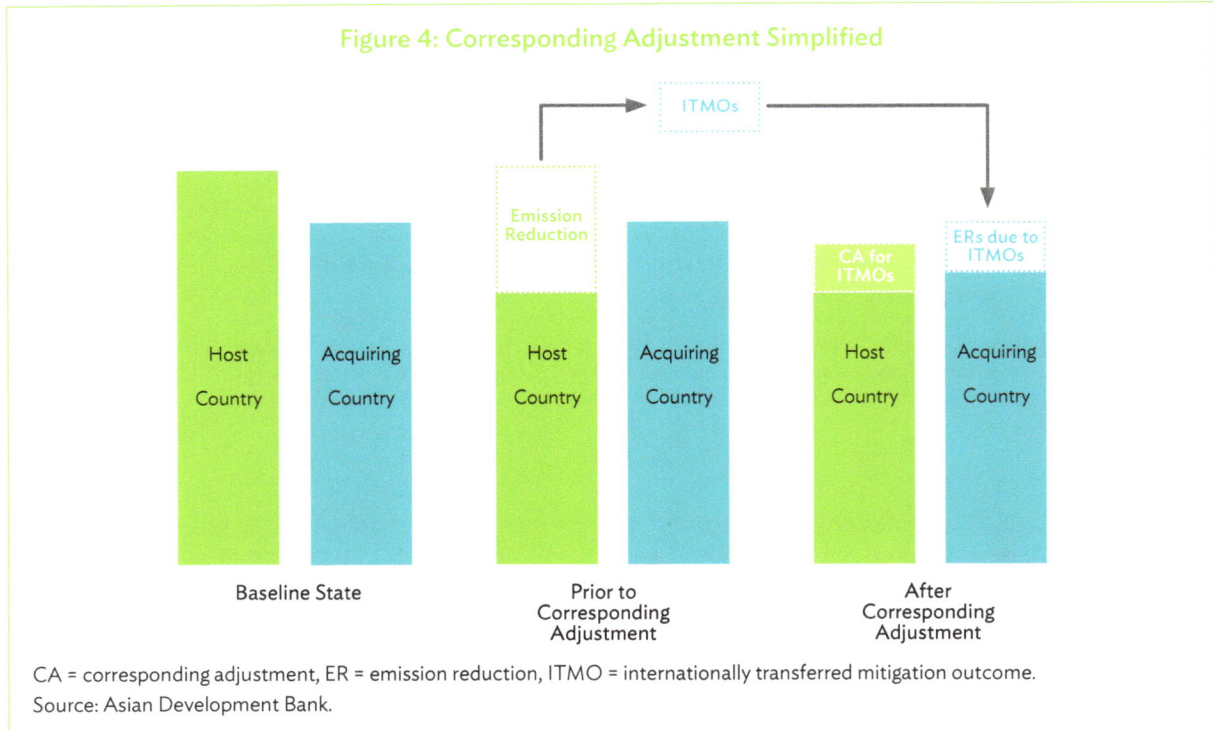

Figure 4: Corresponding Adjustment Simplified

CA = corresponding adjustment, ER = emission reduction, ITMO = internationally transferred mitigation outcome.
Source: Asian Development Bank.

How ITMOs can be reflected in the national inventories under the NDCs involves three discussions: the reporting process, what the corresponding adjustments would be made against, and dealing with corresponding adjustments for ITMOs that are issued annually when a country's NDC target, to be submitted every 5 years, is a single-year basis.[14]

Methods for corresponding adjustment. There is still some obscurity on the discussion of what the corresponding adjustments will be made against, including whether it should be emissions-based (adjustments to national inventories), target- based (adjustment to NDC), or another approach to be taken.

Whichever method may prevail, ultimately, the corresponding adjustment will be made against the country's achievement of its NDC target.

Single vs multiple year targets. According to the UNFCCC Secretariat, most countries communicated single-year targets for 2030, some communicated multiple target years such as 2025 and 2030, and a few countries indicated having a multi-year target for NDC implementation.[15]

Where the participating Party has a single-year NDC target, it can either

(i)   provide a multi-year emissions trajectory so that it can annually apply the corresponding adjustments for ITMOs first transferred; or

(ii) calculate the ITMOs that are to be measured based on methodologies and metrics adopted by the CMA or in other metrics that are consistent with the NDCs.

---

[14] ADB. 2020. *Decoding Article 6 of the Paris Agreement Version II.* Manila.
[15] Conference of the Parties Serving as the Meeting of the Parties to the Paris Agreement. 2021. *Nationally Determined Contributions under the Paris Agreement–Synthesis Report by the Secretariat,* FCCC/PA/CMA/2021/2 (26 February).

As a simplified example, let us look at a group of Article 6.2 activities that reduces around 11 MtCO$_2$e/year every year between 2026 and 2030, with that mitigation outcome being shared equally between the host country and acquiring country (Table 3).

Table 3: Simplified Example of Application of Corresponding Adjustment

Case A: Expected NDC performance (gradual increase)

	Emission Reductions		Progress of NDC (from BAU)		Corresponding Adjustment		Net Progress of NDC (from BAU)	
	Total	As ITMOs	Single Year	Multi Year	Single Year	Multi Year	Single Year	Multi Year
2026	10,000,000	5,000,000		(770,000,000)		5,000,000		(765,000,000)
2027	11,000,000	5,500,000		(780,000,000)		5,500,000		(774,500,000)
2028	10,500,000	5,250,000		(800,000,000)		5,250,000		(794,750,000)
2029	12,000,000	6,000,000		(820,000,000)		6,000,000		(814,000,000)
2030	10,000,000	5,000,000	(850,000,000)	(850,000,000)	5,350,000	5,000,000	(844,650,000)	(845,000,000)
Total	**53,500,000**	**26,750,000**						
Average	**10,700,000**	**5,350,000**	**(850,000,000)**	**(804,000,000)**			**(844,650,000)**	**(798,650,000)**

Case B: Unexpectedly bad NDC performance in reporting year

	Emission Reductions		Progress of NDC (from BAU)		Corresponding Adjustment		Net Progress of NDC (from BAU)	
	Total	As ITMOs	Single Year	Multi Year	Single Year	Multi Year	Single Year	Multi Year
2026	10,000,000	5,000,000		(760,000,000)		5,000,000		(755,000,000)
2027	11,000,000	5,500,000		(800,000,000)		5,500,000		(794,500,000)
2028	10,500,000	5,250,000		(830,000,000)		5,250,000		(824,750,000)
2029	12,000,000	6,000,000		(840,000,000)		6,000,000		(834,000,000)
2030	10,000,000	5,000,000	(800,000,000)	(800,000,000)	5,350,000	5,000,000	(794,650,000)	(795,000,000)
Total	**53,500,000**	**26,750,000**						
Average	**10,700,000**	**5,350,000**	**(800,000,000)**	**(806,000,000)**			**(794,650,000)**	**(800,650,000)**

BAU = business as usual, ITMO = internationally transferred mitigation outcome, NDC = nationally determined contribution.
Source: Asian Development Bank.

Concerns over corresponding adjustment. At a national and international level, several concerns are present:

(i)   Whether the partner country's reference year emission levels, against which the NDC target for reductions is set, are overstated (See footnote 9).

(ii) Whether there needs to be safeguards such as stopping the transfer of ITMOs if a country (or relevant sector of the country) cannot meet its NDC target; moreover, how to weigh up and design responses to a national-level issue of failing to meet an NDC target, when refusing to approve an ITMO ultimately affects a project participant.[16]

(iii) Distinction between conditional and unconditional targets. Some advocate that corresponding adjustments and therefore ITMOs should only occur to emission reductions above and beyond unconditional NDC targets, while others reject this as potentially driving away investors to mitigation activities.

These are not issues that the JCM can resolve. Nevertheless, active dialogue about them between the partnering countries will facilitate operationalization.

---

[16] R. Spalding-Fecher et al. 2020. *Practical Strategies to Avoid Over-selling—Final Report.*

2.6 Reporting

Guidance on reporting requirements is long and not reproduced here.

The Draft Article 6.2 Rulebook states reporting requirements including demonstration of participation responsibilities. Reporting requirements include

(i)   communication and maintenance of an NDC,
(ii)   having arrangements in place for authorizing the use of ITMOs toward NDCs,
(iii)   having arrangements in place for tracking ITMOs, and
(iv)   providing the most recent national inventory report.

The Draft Article 6.2 Rulebook also indicates that there will be an "Article 6 database" implemented by the UNFCCC Secretariat as part of the centralized accounting and reporting platform. When fully connected in future, information on Article 6.2 ITMOs is expected to be published in a centralized accounting and reporting platform maintained by the UNFCCC Secretariat.

These requirements are beyond the purview of the JCM and not discussed in this paper, except to state two interrelated points. One is that these requirements are presumed to be fulfilled in ensuing discussions regarding the operationalization of Article 6.2 in relation to the JCM. The other is that both acquiring and host countries will need to report on the mitigation outcomes from an Article 6.2 mechanism in a different manner as before in their communications to the UNFCCC. The different manner of reporting affects host countries more than it does acquiring countries, the latter of which traditionally consisted of industrialized countries that already had similar reporting requirements under the Kyoto Protocol. New requirements that particularly affect host countries under the Paris Agreement include submission of an emission balance that is adjusted for corresponding adjustments, and submission of information on how each Article 6.1 mechanism promotes sustainable development, ensures environmental integrity and transparency including in governance, applies robust accounting to ensure inter alia the avoidance of double counting.[17]

---

[17] Conference of the Parties Serving as the Meeting of the Parties to the Paris Agreement. 2019. *Report of the Conference of the Parties Serving as the Meeting of the Parties to the Paris Agreement on the Third Part of its First Session, Held in Katowice from 2 to 15 December 2018–Addendum–Part Two: Action Taken by the Conference of the Parties Serving as the Meeting of the Parties to the Paris Agreement,* FCCC/PA/CMA/2018/3/Add.2 (19 March).

3 Matching Joint Crediting Mechanism Experiences to the Paris Agreement

The JCM is one of the very few existing project-based cooperative approaches, if not the only one, formalized with partner governments, that bears resemblance to what an operationalized Article 6.2 mechanism will look like.

By looking at the current level of JCM alignment and compatibility to the cooperative approaches as described under the Draft Article 6.2 Rulebook, this section seeks to highlight lessons learned that are broadly generalizable to what it takes to implement a 6.2 mechanism.

3.1 Real and Verified Emission Reductions

Under the JCM, an approved methodology is employed to calculate emission reductions achieved by each project and to determine the post-implementation monitoring plan.

Figure 5: Joint Crediting Mechanism Project Cycle to Validation and Registration

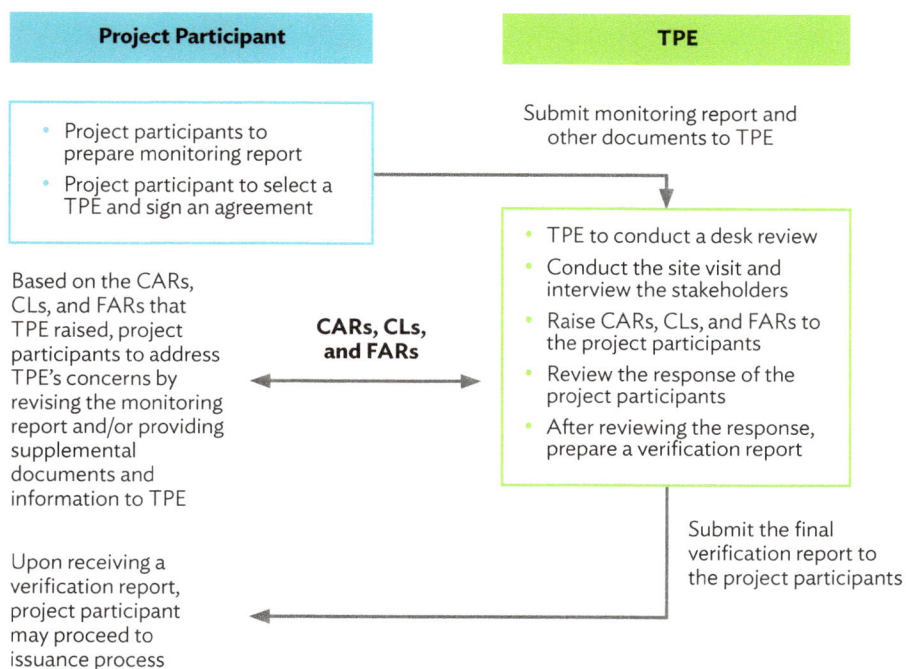

Project Participant	TPE
• Project participants to prepare monitoring report • Project participant to select a TPE and sign an agreement	Submit monitoring report and other documents to TPE
Based on the CARs, CLs, and FARs that TPE raised, project participants to address TPE's concerns by revising the monitoring report and/or providing supplemental documents and information to TPE	• TPE to conduct a desk review • Conduct the site visit and interview the stakeholders • Raise CARs, CLs, and FARs to the project participants • Review the response of the project participants • After reviewing the response, prepare a verification report
Upon receiving a verification report, project participant may proceed to issuance process	Submit the final verification report to the project participants

CARs, CLs, and FARs

CAR = corrective action request, CL = clarification request, FAR = forward action request, TPE = third-party entity.
Source: Asian Development Bank.

Drawing from the lessons of the CDM with its oftentimes complex methodologies, JCM methodologies employ simple and conservative methods. Streamlining is achieved by requiring the JCM methodology to be accompanied by a template spreadsheet with pre-approved default factors already contained where necessary.

The default factors and emission factors contained in the methodology and accompanying spreadsheets are approved by the bilateral Joint Committee. Therefore, for the exact same activity (e.g., installation of an energy-efficient refrigerator model X) carried out in two countries A and B, the methodologies employed may be different depending on national circumstances such as the respective grid emission factor and the input from the Joint Committees for countries A and B.

Similar to the CDM, third-party validation and verification is carried out by an independent auditor, i.e., third-party entities (TPEs) to ensure that the emission reductions are "real" and "verified." Figure 5 shows the JCM project cycle to validation and registration showing when TPEs are involved. TPEs are either to be accredited under ISO 14065 or be existing Designated Operations Entities under the CDM. These TPEs are also approved by the Joint Committee, allowing non-international auditors to validate and verify projects armed with intimate knowledge of the local situation.

3.2   Additional Emission Reductions

Unlike the CDM, which separates the determination of baseline emission levels and determination of additional emission reductions, the JCM has deliberately adopted what could be considered a more robust method to ascertain additionality. The JCM's basic position is to establish reference emission levels conservatively by setting it below the BAU level (Figure 6).

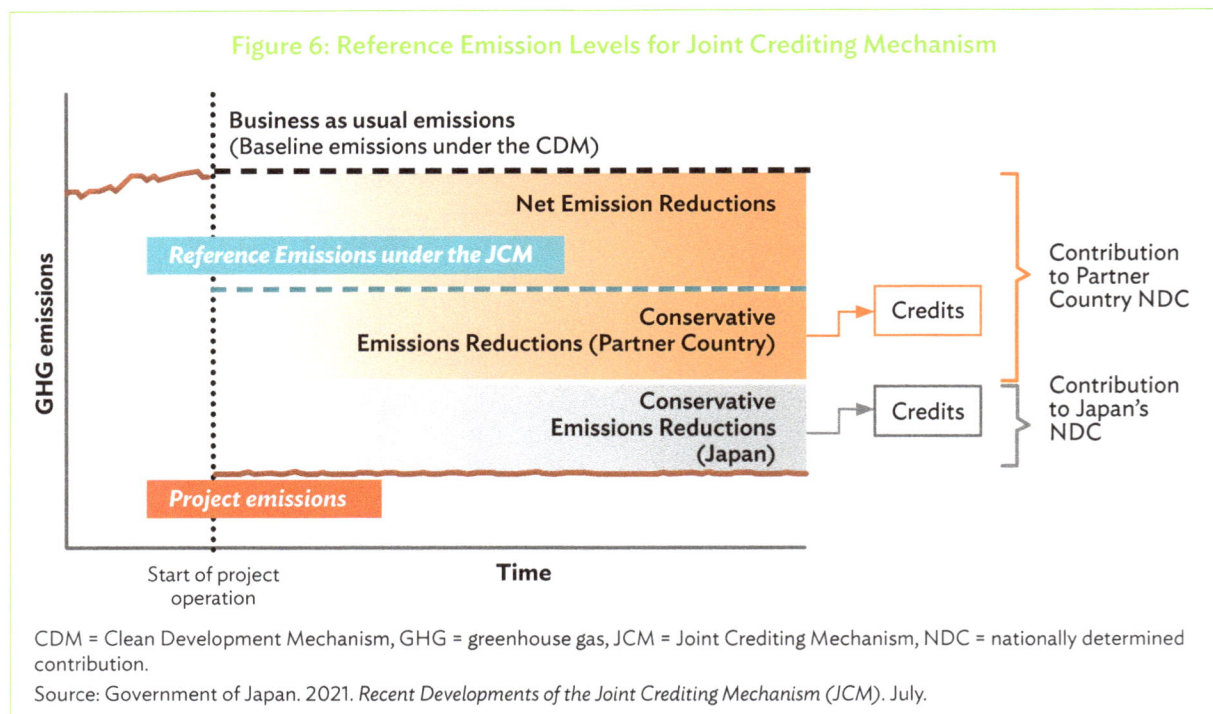

Figure 6: Reference Emission Levels for Joint Crediting Mechanism

CDM = Clean Development Mechanism, GHG = greenhouse gas, JCM = Joint Crediting Mechanism, NDC = nationally determined contribution.
Source: Government of Japan. 2021. *Recent Developments of the Joint Crediting Mechanism (JCM)*. July.

Under the JCM, the method to quantify reference emission levels and thus the additional emission reductions is carried out as part of the methodology development and approval cycle, and approved by the bilateral Joint Committee to reflect individual partner country circumstances. However, such reference emissions currently do not take national ambitions set in the NDC of the partner country into consideration.

Exactly how a reference emission level for mitigation activities under an Article 6.2 mechanism can align with the NDC target is a topic that requires further and careful discussion among stakeholders. The ease of achieving alignment will also vary from country to country. For instance, one host country may have targets for each sector it reports (e.g., 30% overall reduction consisting of 10% from energy, 10% from land use, land-use change and forestry, etc.) enabling discussions on NDC alignment to start at that sector target, while another country may only have a single target for its overall emission (e.g., 30% overall reduction) which makes the discussion more difficult. Other hurdles such as questions over a reference level at a particular point in time during the NDC reporting period are also present.

Given the complex nature of determining additional emission reductions in relation to each country's NDC targets, it could be argued that the JCM approach to (a) base the determination on reference emission levels, and (b) to take a bilateral approach to jointly approve that reference level as appropriate, makes it closer to achieving operationalization of Article 6.2 than other alternatives.

3.3 Authorization

Under the JCM, the Joint Committee performs all final approval functions. The Joint Committee, set up between Japan and each partner country, is a bilateral committee consisting of representatives from both governments. In addition to performing various other functions, the Joint Committee approves each project, in the forms of Registration (formal acceptance of a validated project) and Issuance of JCM credits (formal acceptance of third-party-verified results).

Between the registration and issuance under the current JCM project cycle, approval of issuance is the one that is equivalent to authorization under Article 6.2, which focuses on authorizing the *international transfer* of mitigation outcomes.

Registration. Registration is the formal acceptance of participation as a JCM project. Once the project participants have conducted local stakeholder consultation and have received a positive validation opinion from the TPE, the project participants may submit their project design document, validation report, Modalities of Communication, and a completed JCM Project Registration Request Form to the secretariat to officially request registration (Figure 7).

Issuance. JCM credits will be issued based on the results and findings of the verification report containing monitored data. Upon receiving the verification report from the TPE, the project participants request the issuance of credits by submitting a Credits Issuance Request Form, information on the allocation of credits among the project participants, the verified monitoring report, and the verification report to the Joint Committee through the secretariat (Figure 8).

The concept of the Joint Committee with relevant government representatives jointly approving a JCM project is in alignment with Article 6.2.

Figure 7: Joint Crediting Mechanism Registration Process

Project Participant	Secretariat	Joint Committee

Project participants to submit JCM Project Registration Request Form, PDD, validation report, MOC, and other supplemental documents

Develop a proposed methodology under the Initiative of the Joint Committee

Editorial Issues

Project participants and TPE to revise and submit the requested document (7 calendar days)

Conduct completeness check (7 calendar days)

Incomplete — Complete

Make the final decision
(a) Register
(b) Reject

Project participant/ TPE may further revise the documents and resubmit a new request

Notify project participants and TPE, and make the final decision made by the Joint Committee publicly available

Rejected

Proceed with projects, implementation and monitoring

Registered

JCM = Joint Crediting Mechanism, MOC = modalities of communication statement, PDD = project design document, TPE = third-party entity.
Source: Asian Development Bank.

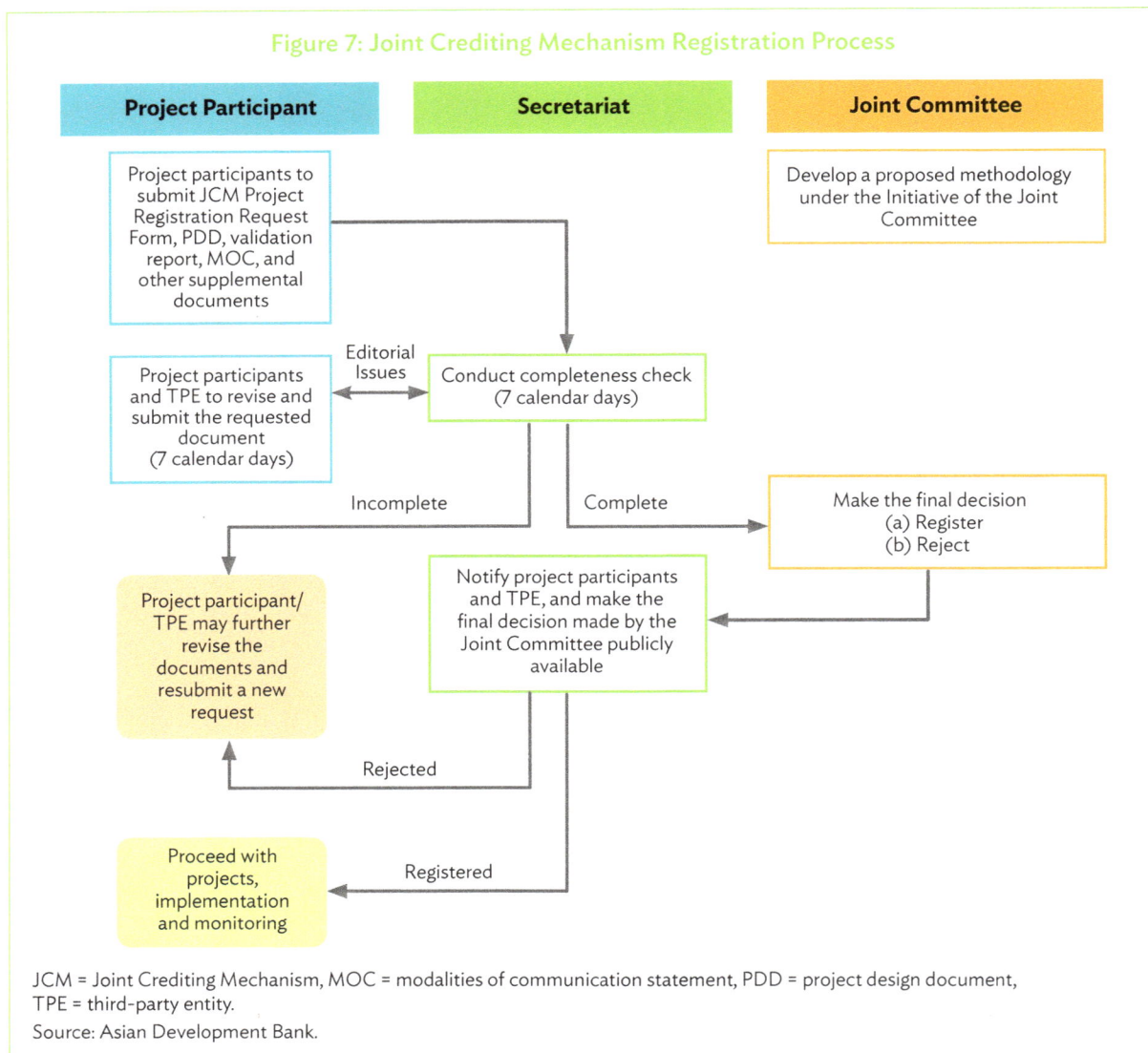

However, as the bilateral agreements were drawn up prior to the Paris Agreement, authorization of ITMOs is not dealt with in the current agreements and it is not clear how the authorization will be granted. The JCM could modify or set up a bilateral committee that has the mandate to authorize an ITMO whether by having the committee entrusted to directly authorize or by having the authorization channeled through the committee. It is also possible that governments will instead opt to have a centralized authorization body that will oversee Article 6.2 and other international carbon transactions, including expanding the existing Designated National Authority (DNA) for CDM/JI to perform the same function. While a case-by-case approach to alignment is therefore likely necessary for the JCM, partner countries have already gained knowledge and experience in authorizing bilateral approach activities.

Figure 8: Joint Crediting Mechanism Credit Issuance Process

Project Participant	Secretariat	Joint Committee

- Project participants to open up account in the registry of Japan and/or host country
- Project participants to submit JCM Credits Issuance Request Form, Monitoring Report, Verification Report, and other supplemental documents

Editorial Issues

Project participants and TPE to revise and submit the requested document (7 calendar days)

Conduct completeness check (7 calendar days)

Incomplete — **Complete**

Make the final decision
(a) Register
(b) Reject

Project participant/ TPE may further revise the documents and resubmit a new request

Notify project participants and TPE, and make the final decision made by the Joint Committee publicly available

Proceed with projects, implementation and monitoring

Rejected

Credits to be issued

Government of Japan/Host country government

- Issue the JCM credits to the respective registry accounts
- Notify the Joint Committee/ secretariat of the issuance

JCM = Joint Crediting Mechanism, TPE = third-party entity.
Source: Asian Development Bank.

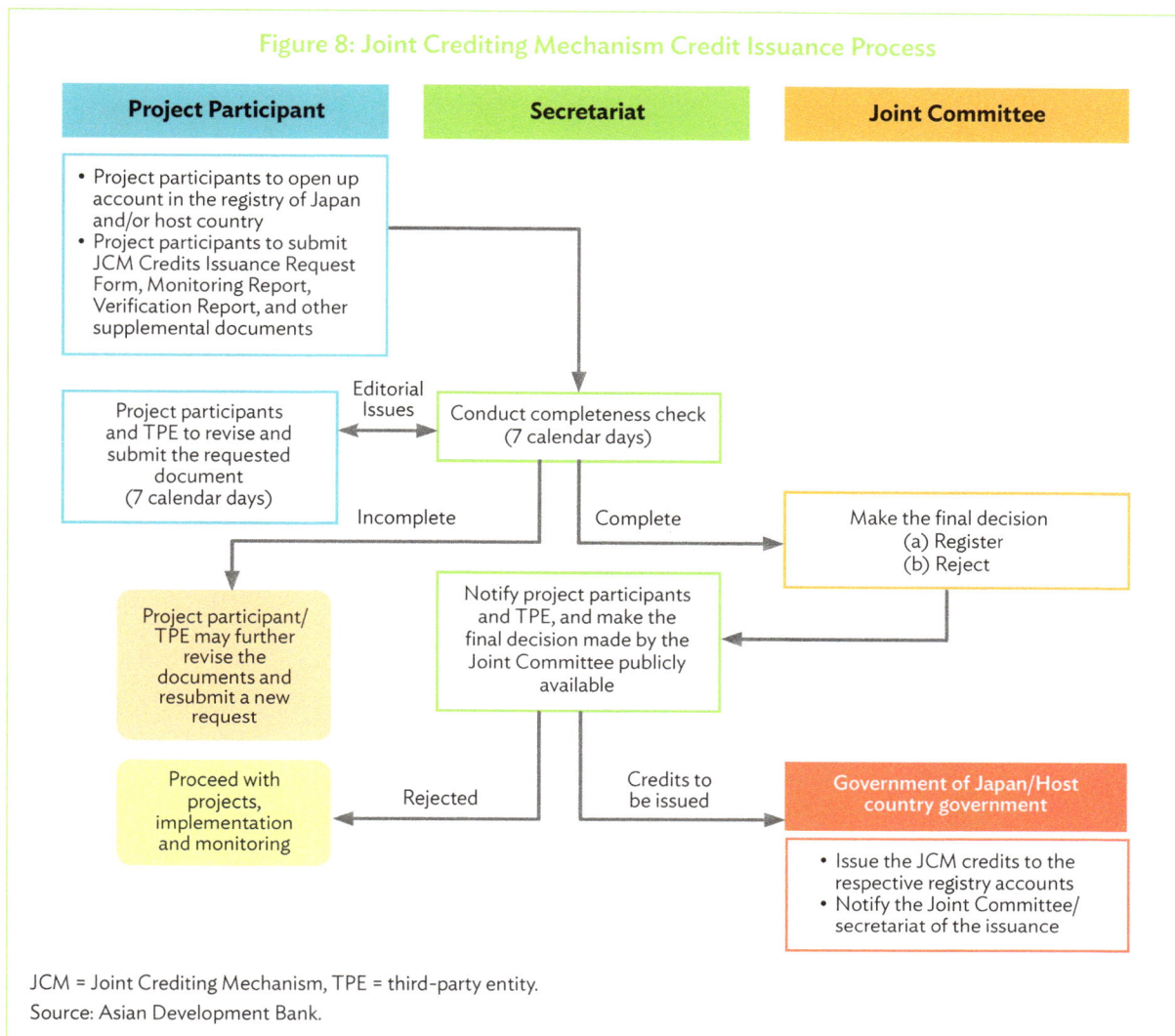

A possible DNA-like body could look like Figure 9, wherein, as an example:

(i)   A mechanism X will assess projects within its joint committee, with the host country side of the joint committee having the authority to also conduct checks on ITMOs as described in Section 2.1.4. Authorization for Article 6.2 purposes will be conducted by the joint committees and the national authorizing authority will be notified of such result.

(ii)   A mechanism Y will take the path in between X and Z, where the host country side of the joint committee will authorize ITMOs in close consultation with the national authorizing authority.

(iii)   A mechanism Z will not take the role of authorizing projects for Article 6.2 purposes. The projects will be checked for compliance to mechanism Z standards, but for authorization of ITMOs its joint committee will only act as an official conduit to the national authorizing authority, with the latter carrying out the checks and authorization.

(iv)   Article 6.2 pilot programs will request ITMO authorization from the national authority.

As experience is gained, countries that started off with several paths to authorization may streamline them to one path, or vice versa.

Figure 9: Possible Future Article 6.2 Authorizations

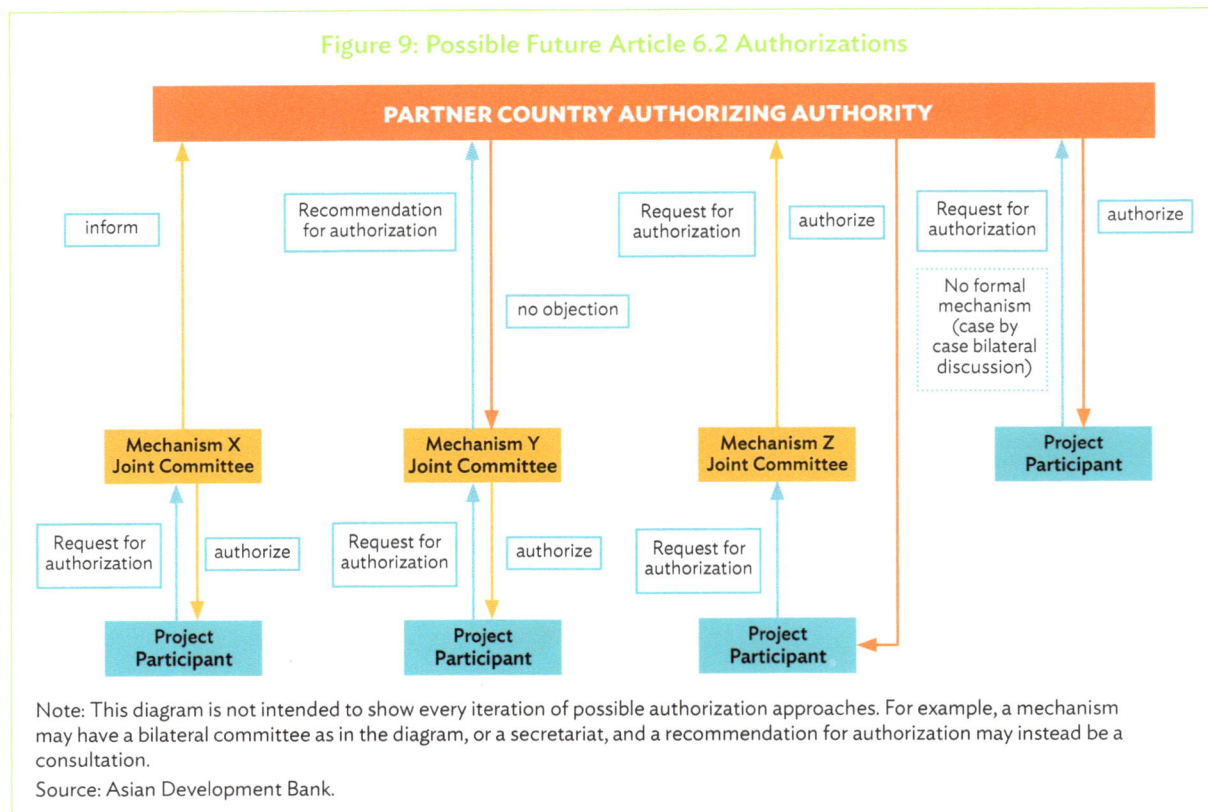

PARTNER COUNTRY AUTHORIZING AUTHORITY

inform | Recommendation for authorization | Request for authorization | authorize | Request for authorization | authorize

no objection

No formal mechanism (case by case bilateral discussion)

Mechanism X Joint Committee | Mechanism Y Joint Committee | Mechanism Z Joint Committee | Project Participant

Request for authorization | authorize | Request for authorization | authorize | Request for authorization

Project Participant | Project Participant | Project Participant

Note: This diagram is not intended to show every iteration of possible authorization approaches. For example, a mechanism may have a bilateral committee as in the diagram, or a secretariat, and a recommendation for authorization may instead be a consultation.
Source: Asian Development Bank.

3.4 Sustainable Development

Sustainable development is a core principle of the JCM, which supports the transition to low-carbon and decarbonization societies through advanced technologies.

Under the JCM bilateral agreements, the partner country can develop its own environmental and sustainable development criteria for the JCM approval process, as is the case for Indonesia and Mongolia. This allows the partner country full ownership to set criteria for JCM projects to match their own sustainable development goals. This is a positive attribute of the JCM and in alignment with the specific stated aim of Article 6.2. The existing JCM framework that enables partner countries to develop and/or further elaborate its own criteria can be actively encouraged with existing and future partner countries.

3.5 Avoidance of Double Counting

The JCM was conceived as a mechanism outside of the Kyoto Protocol with a view to not only providing an alternative to the CDM, but with the evolution of the international cooperation on mitigation efforts firmly in mind from the start. Double counting is avoided in the existing JCM framework by

(i)   "sharing" the JCM credits via formal agreement at the individual project level between the governments of Japan and the partner country and project participants, and

(ii)   having a system of JCM registries in both Japan and the partner country.

The JCM itself already has sufficient safeguards against double counting which builds foundation for further alignment with Article 6.2 and ensuring development of a corresponding adjustment mechanism connecting the JCM registry and the NDC achievements. Figure 10 shows the link between having a JCM registry and corresponding adjustments. A mechanism to report the occurrence of ITMOs to initiate the application of corresponding adjustments—as distinct from the application of the corresponding adjustments itself—to the partner country NDC needs to be agreed and added as an extra step.

Figure 10: Link between Joint Crediting Mechanism Registry and Corresponding Adjustments

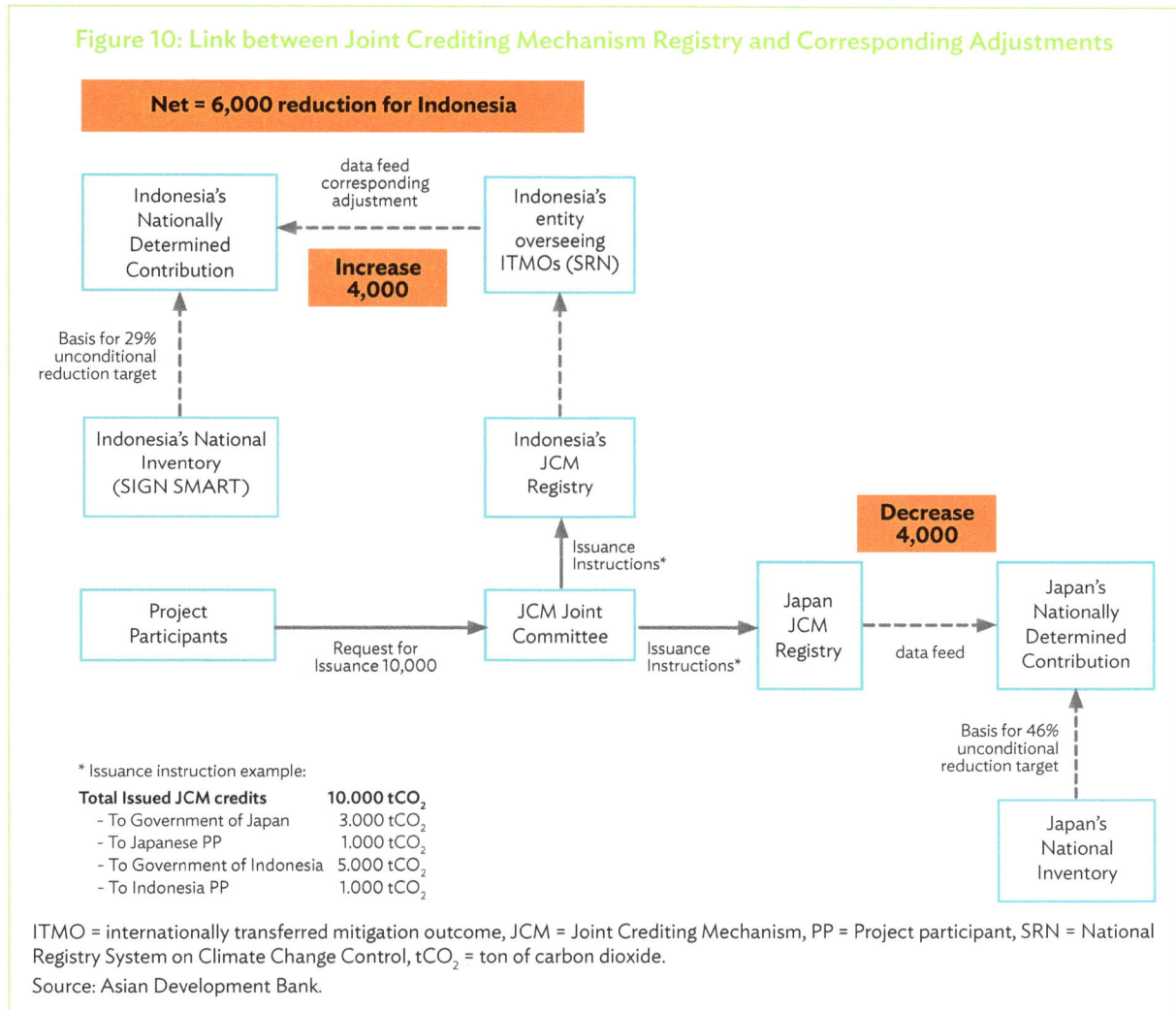

Net = 6,000 reduction for Indonesia

data feed corresponding adjustment

Indonesia's Nationally Determined Contribution

Increase 4,000

Indonesia's entity overseeing ITMOs (SRN)

Basis for 29% unconditional reduction target

Indonesia's National Inventory (SIGN SMART)

Indonesia's JCM Registry

Project Participants

Request for Issuance 10,000

JCM Joint Committee

Issuance Instructions*

Issuance Instructions*

Japan JCM Registry

data feed

Decrease 4,000

Japan's Nationally Determined Contribution

Basis for 46% unconditional reduction target

Japan's National Inventory

* Issuance instruction example:

Total Issued JCM credits	10.000 tCO$_2$
– To Government of Japan	3.000 tCO$_2$
– To Japanese PP	1.000 tCO$_2$
– To Government of Indonesia	5.000 tCO$_2$
– To Indonesia PP	1.000 tCO$_2$

ITMO = internationally transferred mitigation outcome, JCM = Joint Crediting Mechanism, PP = Project participant, SRN = National Registry System on Climate Change Control, tCO$_2$ = ton of carbon dioxide.
Source: Asian Development Bank.

Further rules are expected to emerge from future Subsidiary Body for Scientific and Technological Advice meetings in relation to ITMOs, including on the timing of corresponding adjustments.

3.6 Reporting

Reporting requirements for ITMOs are imposed on Parties at the national level and is beyond the purview of the JCM.

Figure 11 below briefly explains the existing reporting mechanisms for issued JCM credits.

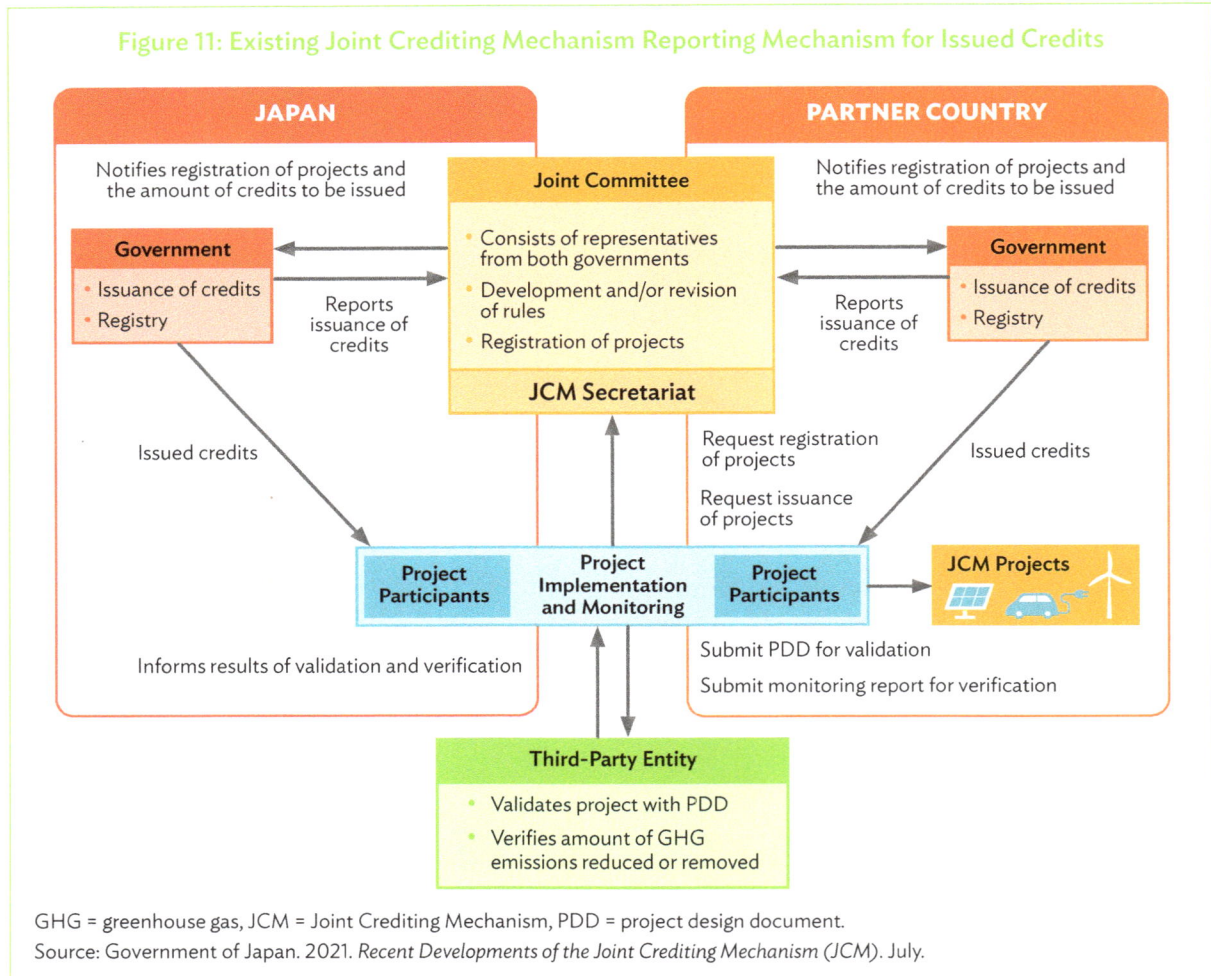

Figure 11: Existing Joint Crediting Mechanism Reporting Mechanism for Issued Credits

JAPAN

Notifies registration of projects and the amount of credits to be issued

Government
- Issuance of credits
- Registry

Reports issuance of credits

Joint Committee
- Consists of representatives from both governments
- Development and/or revision of rules
- Registration of projects

JCM Secretariat

PARTNER COUNTRY

Notifies registration of projects and the amount of credits to be issued

Government
- Issuance of credits
- Registry

Reports issuance of credits

Issued credits

Request registration of projects

Request issuance of projects

Issued credits

Project Participants — **Project Implementation and Monitoring** — **Project Participants** — **JCM Projects**

Informs results of validation and verification

Submit PDD for validation

Submit monitoring report for verification

Third-Party Entity
- Validates project with PDD
- Verifies amount of GHG emissions reduced or removed

GHG = greenhouse gas, JCM = Joint Crediting Mechanism, PDD = project design document.
Source: Government of Japan. 2021. *Recent Developments of the Joint Crediting Mechanism (JCM).* July.

Japan has a JCM registry already established since November 2015 that is linked to its national inventory (Figure 12).

Each of the partner countries are to also establish their own registry.

Between the Japanese JCM registry and the partner country JCM registry, which share common specifications, all JCM credits are fully accounted for and allocated according to the sharing agreement.

In that the JCM already has a full-fledged reporting system, it is able to immediately provide all requisite JCM-related data in order for each partner country to meet its reporting obligations. Data flows can be discussed and arranged to flow to the partner country national inventory.

Figure 12: Joint Crediting Mechanism Registry for Japan

JCM = Joint Crediting Mechanism, JST = Japan standard time, GMT = Greenwich Mean Time.
Source: The Joint Crediting Mechanism Registry System.

4 Joint Crediting Mechanism Partner Countries and the Paris Agreement

In this section, how the JCM is aligned to Article 6.2 is examined at a country level, using Indonesia as an example. Doing so demonstrates the processes countries have already developed or implemented that can be used as a stepping stone when utilizing future bilateral market mechanisms as envisaged under Article 6.2 of the Paris Agreement.

Indonesia was chosen since it is the JCM partner country with the largest track record of JCM projects. Importantly, the Government of Indonesia has taken an active interest in taking advance action in being a forerunner for operationalizing Article 6.2, as highlighted in their most recent NDC. Indonesia also has a fully functioning JCM registry in addition to its other advanced registry systems, and has also adopted its own sustainable development criteria for the purpose of JCM project approvals, providing useful insight to other countries.

Indonesia and Japan started discussing and negotiating JCM cooperation in 2010, back then still named as the Bilateral Offset Crediting Mechanism, and in August 2013, the Government of Indonesia and the Government of Japan signed a bilateral cooperation agreement on the JCM. The first JCM Indonesia project registered was in October 2014 and the issuance of the first credit was in May 2016.

As of August 2021, there are 23 projects registered under the JCM in Indonesia with a total mitigation potential of around 44,500 tCO_2/year. There have been 12 projects issued with 56,254 JCM credits in total, with 35% issued for the Indonesian side.

Again, these six elements are assessed in the ensuing sections.

(i)   Real and verified emission reductions
(ii) Additional emission reductions
(iii) Authorization
(iv) Sustainable development
(v)   Avoidance of double counting
(vi) Reporting

4.1 Real and Verified Emission Reductions

The JCM framework ensures real and verified emission reductions in a manner in full compliance with Article 6.2. Indonesia's JCM requires validation and verification of individual projects by TPEs.

Indonesia has nine approved TPEs authorized to validate and verify emission reductions as of September 2021. The Indonesian JCM Joint Committee has, to date, authorized the issuance of 56,254 tCO_2e of real and verified emission reductions.

4.2 Additional Emission Reductions

According to Joint Crediting Mechanism Guidelines for Developing Proposed Methodology, for Indonesian JCM projects, reference emissions should be below BAU emissions and can be calculated either through discounting BAU emissions or through other means that will be determined in methodologies which will need to be approved by the Joint Committee.[18]

The method to quantify reference emission levels and emission reductions is based on JCM methodologies approved for each partner country to accurately reflect the local circumstances. Indonesia has approved 28 JCM methodologies to date.

What this precisely transfers to at a mechanism or project level is to be determined. Nevertheless, for Indonesia, a starting point in moving forward with the discussion on reference emission levels will be the unconditional NDC targets. Indonesia has set an unconditional reduction target from its projected 2030 BAU emission levels. The emission levels projection started in 2010 and is expected to reach 2.87 $GtCO_2e$ in 2030 under BAU.[19] Thus, the unconditional reduction target of 29% translates to a reduction of 0.83 $GtCO_2$, equivalent to a net emission level of 2.04 $GtCO_2e$.

Further, when the sector targets are reviewed, the unconditional sectoral target for energy is 18.8% and for waste 3.7%[20] (uncorrected for annual average growth) (Table 4). Where there are sector targets such as these, it would make sense for these to be taken into consideration over national targets for the setting of the reference level.

Table 4: Projected Business as Usual and Emission Reduction from Each Sector/Category in Indonesia

Sector	GHG Emission Level 2010[a] (MtCO_2e)	GHG Emission Level 2030 MtCO_2e			GHG Emission Reduction MtCO_2e		GHG Emission Reduction % of Total BAU		Annual Average Growth BAU (2010–2030)	Average Growth 2000–2012
		BAU	CM1	CM2	CM1	CM2	CM1	CM2		
1. Energy[a]	453.2	1,669	1,355	1,223	314	446	11%	15.5%	6.7%	4.50%
2. Waste	88	296	285	256	11	40	0.38%	1.4%	6.3%	4.00%
3. IPPU	36	70	67	66	3	3.25	0.10%	0.11%	3.4%	0.10%
4. Agriculture[b]	111	120	110	116	9	4	0.32%	0.13%	0.4%	1.30%
5. Forestry and Other Land Uses (FOLU)[c]	647	714	217	22	497	692	17.2%	24.1%	0.5%	2.70%
TOTAL	1,334	2,869	2,034	1,683	834	1,185	29%	41%	3.9%	3.20%

Notes: CM1 = Counter Measure 1 (*unconditional mitigation scenario*)
CM2 = Counter Measure 2 (*conditional mitigation scenario*)

[a] Including fugitive.
[b] Only include rice cultivation and livestock.
[c] Including emission from estate crops plantation.

BAU = business as usual, GHG = greenhouse gas, IPPU = industrial processes and product use, $MtCO_2e$ = metric tons of carbon dioxide equivalent.

Source: Government of Indonesia. 2021. *Updated Nationally Determined Contribution*. Jakarta.

---

[18] JCM. *Joint Crediting Mechanism Guidelines for Developing Proposed Methodology*.
[19] R. Boer et al. 2018. Indonesia Second Biennial Update Report under the United Nations Framework Convention on Climate Change. Jakarta: Directorate General of Climate Change, Ministry of Environment and Forestry.
[20] For example, for the energy sector, the BAU emission level for 2030 is estimated to be 1,669 metric tons of carbon dioxide equivalent ($MtCO_2e$) and the unconditional reduction target is 314 $MtCO_2e$, representing an 18.8% unconditional reduction target for the sector.

How exactly to do so is the discussion that needs to be initiated for alignment with Article 6.2, which itself is silent on methods, as stated in Section 3.1.3. Continuing with the example of the energy sector, the first point would be to understand the basis of the 314 $MtCO_2e$ target and how the partner government intends to meet the target from actions within the energy sector, which can range from transitioning to lower-carbon intensity fuels (imports and/or production), adding renewable energy capacity, and rehabilitating old conventional plants (improved efficiency). When such breakdowns are not available, a question may be asked whether a blunt method such as a blanket application of the sector target (18.8% in the case of Indonesia) to current practice emissions be adopted as reference emission level for all JCM energy sector projects regardless of what that measure is. The issue of quantifying additional emission reductions is an important issue in moving forward with Article 6.2.

4.3 Authorization

Approval for the JCM is provided by the bilateral Joint Committee, which consists of representatives from various sections of government (Table 5).

Table 5: Representatives of Indonesia's Joint Crediting Mechanism Joint Committee

Members	Affiliation (Position)
Joint Committee members representing Indonesia	Coordinating Ministry for Economic Affairs (Assistant Deputy Minister for Multilateral Economic Cooperation)
	Coordinating Ministry for Economic Affairs (Assistant Deputy Minister for Agro, Pharmacy and Tourism)
	Ministry of Environment and Forestry (Director of Sectoral and Regional Resource Mobilization)
	Ministry of Environment and Forestry (Head of Research and Development Center for Social, Economic, Policy, and Climate Change)
	Ministry of Energy and Mineral Resources (Director of Various New Energy and Renewable Energy)
	Ministry of Industry (Head of Centre for Green Industry)
	Ministry of National Development Planning/Bappenas (Director for the Environment)
	Ministry of Finance (Acting Head of Policy Center for Climate Change and Financing and Multilateral)
	Ministry of Foreign Affairs (Director for Economic Development and Environment)
Joint Committee members representing Japan	Embassy of Japan in Indonesia
	Ministry of Foreign Affairs
	Ministry of Economy, Trade and Industry
	Ministry of the Environment
	Forestry Agency

Source: JCM Indonesia Secretariat. Joint Committee.

The Joint Committee develops the rules and guidelines of the JCM, designates the third-party entities to conduct validation and/or verification under the JCM, registers validated JCM projects, notifies issuance of credits, develops the JCM operation report, and conducts policy consultations.

In accordance with the Rules of Procedures for the Joint Committee, the Joint Committee will meet as necessary but no less than once a year, whether in person, by electronic means, or by conference call. Decisions by the Joint Committee are adopted by consensus, with the co-Chairs ascertaining whether consensus has been reached.[21]

The Joint Committee is supported by the JCM Secretariat, consisting of respective secretariats for Japan and Indonesia (Figure 13). Indonesia's secretariat falls under the Coordinating Ministry for Economic Affairs, which was also signatory of the JCM bilateral agreement.

At the time of preparing this publication, there were no concrete plans as to whether Indonesia will set up a separate authorizing and/or aggregating body for Article 6 purposes.

Indonesia's approval process follows that of the default JCM process. As also discussed under Section 3.1.4, discussions will be necessary between the government of Japan and the government of Indonesia as to how to authorize ITMOs for JCM projects under Article 6.2.

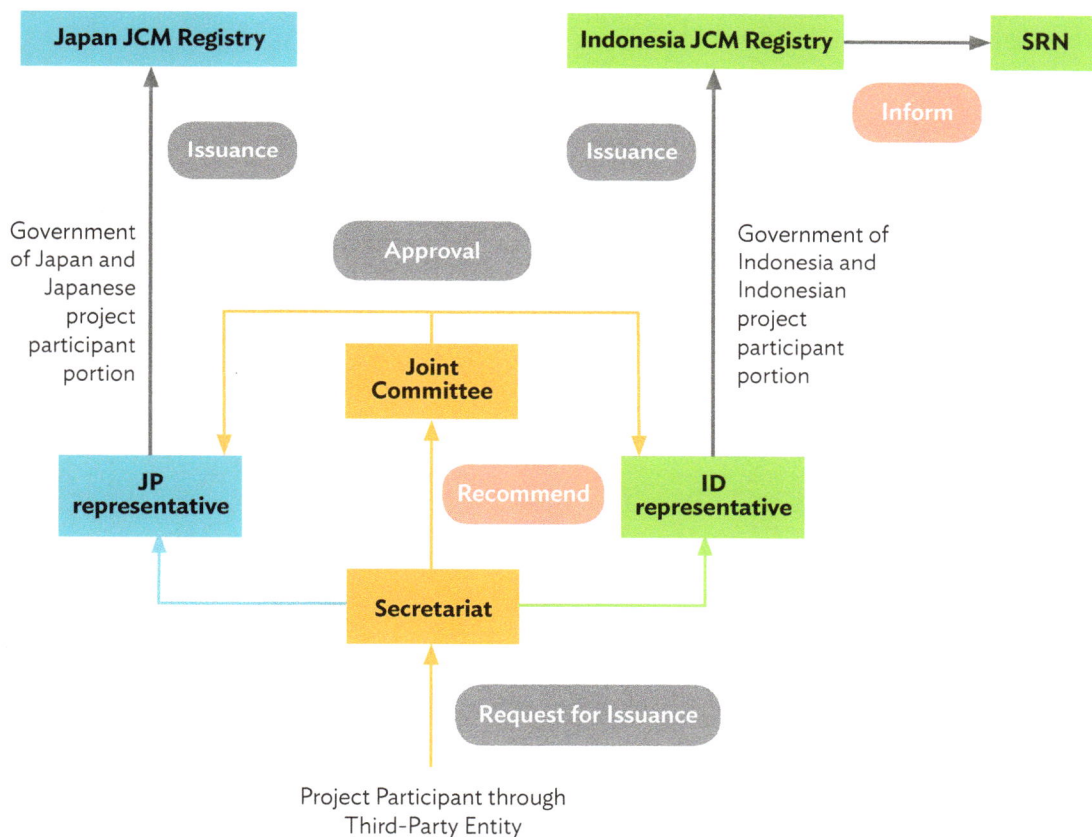

Figure 13: Joint Crediting Mechanism Approval Relationship for Indonesia

ID = Indonesia, JCM = Joint Crediting Mechanism, JP = Japan, SRN = National Registry System on Climate Change Control.
Source: Asian Development Bank.

---

[21] JCM. *Joint Crediting Mechanism Rules of Procedures for the Joint Committee.*

4.4 Sustainable Development

As part of the registration and issuance process, Indonesia requires the JCM project participants to submit a Sustainable Development Implementation Plan and Sustainable Development Implementation Report, respectively.

This is irrespective of the requirements for the completion and submission of an environmental impact assessment or an Analisis Manajemen Dampak Lingkungan—Indonesia (AMDAL) and Environment Management Efforts and Environmental Monitoring Efforts or Usaha Pengelolaan Lingkungan–Usaha Pemantauan Lingkungan (UKL-UPL) that Indonesia already has. An AMDAL is required for any activity that has significant impacts, and UKL–UPL is required for all others, covering most activities that would be implemented under the JCM.[22]

Indonesia's JCM rules requiring the submission of a Sustainable Development Implementation Plan (SDIP) (Table 6), and Sustainable Development Implementation Report (SDIR), despite the assessment criteria significantly overlapping with the AMDAL and UKL–UPL, is in full alignment with Article 6.2.

Table 6: Snapshot of a Sustainable Development Implementation Plan

B. Possible Contribution to Sustainable Development

B.1 Plan for possible contribution to SD

No.	Items	Questions	Yes/No	If answer is Yes, please describe the action plans.
1	EIA	Does the proposed project require official/legal process of EIA?	No	
2	Pollution Control (No need to answer if EIA is required)	Does the proposed project emit air pollutants?	No	
3		Does the proposed project discharge water pollutants or substances which influence BOD, COD or ph, etc.?	No	
4		Does the proposed project generate waste?	Yes	Small amount of waste is expected during the set up of equipment, however, generated waste will be treated in line with the company recycling plan for proper disposal.
5		Does the proposed project increase noise and/or vibration from the current level?	Yes	Certain noise increase is expected, however, proper noise control measure will be carried out.
6		Does the proposed project cause ground subsidence?	No	
7		Does the proposed project cause odor?	No	
8	Safety and health	Does the proposed project create dangerous condition for local communities as well as individuals involved in the project, during either its construction or its operation?	Yes	The project may create a dangerous condition during its installation, however, preventative measures are carried out for securing safety of workers during its installation.
9	Natural Environment and biodiversity	Is the proposed project site located in protected areas designated by national laws or international treaties and conventions?	No	
10		Does the proposed project change land use of the community and protected habitats for endangered species designated by national laws or international treaties and conventions?	No	
11		Does the proposed project bring foreign species?	No	
12		Does the proposed project include construction activities considered to affect natural environment and biodiversity (e.g., noise, vibrations, turbid water, dust, exhaust gases, and wastes)?	No	
13		Does the proposed project use surface water, ground water and/or deep ground water?	No	
14	Economy	Does the proposed project have negative impact on local workforce capacity?	No	

SD = sustainable development, EIA = environmental impact assessment, BOD = biological oxygen demand, COD = chemical oxygen demand.

Source: JCM Indonesia Secretariat. *Joint Crediting Mechanism Guidelines for Developing Sustainable Development Implementation Plan and Report.*

---

[22] Impacts include changing of land and landscape, exploitation of natural resources of both renewable and non-renewable nature, causing pollution or waste, affecting the environment and social and cultural surroundings, affecting natural resources and cultural heritage, among others.

It is also noted that the Institute for Global Environmental Strategies has published the Joint Crediting Mechanism and Sustainable Development Goals Linkage Guidance to support project participants' decision-making toward integrating SDGs into their business, including for new JCM projects. The publication highlights the inherently sustainable nature of JCM projects, which highlights the alignment of this likely criterion for Article 6.2 and provides insights on how this can be satisfied for future projects (Box 6).[23]

Box 6: The Institute for Global Environmental Strategies Joint Crediting Mechanism–Sustainable Development Goals Linkage Guidance

There are 232 indicators of Sustainable Development Goals (SDGs) developed by the United Nations. These indicators are crucial in measuring the global progress of sustainable development (SD). These, however, are naturally not all business-oriented. Understanding and navigating SDG requirements and quantifying achievements can be challenging for all but a minority of well-prepared businesses.

The Joint Crediting Mechanism (JCM)–SDGs linkage guidance outlines both qualitative and quantitative SDG indicators, developed based on a study of the low-carbon technologies adopted in JCM projects in various countries. The linkage guidance maps out SDGs and targets, identifies the linkage of those with the JCM indicators, and further links them to specific JCM project examples. As the linkage can be searched either from the SDGs and targets or from the type of project, this allows project developers to easily search (a) the types of projects that meet the specific SDGs and targets they are interested in achieving, and (b) the SDGs and targets their planned project may meet.

The examples in the linkage guidance show that JCM projects contribute to environment and energy-related SDGs and those with social dimensions including quality education, good health and well-being, and decent work and economic growth. The figure demonstrates the contribution of JCM to achieving SDG targets.

The guidance can be used to quickly assess how JCM projects contribute to SDGs. For project participants, this not

Joint Crediting Mechanism and Sustainable Development Goals

Common SDGs that JCM contributes:
- 4.4 Technical training
- 7.a International cooperation to increase clean energy
- 9.4 Sustainable Industry
- 12.4 Responsible consumption and management of natural resource
- 13.3 Improve employees' awareness of climate change
- 17.3 Mobilizing private capital to support SDGs

Potential JCM projects:
- 1. Renewable energy in irrigation system — To contribute sustainable agriculture and increase efficient water management
- 2. Wastewater treatment — To enhance public health and sanitation; and support sustainable cities
- 3. Solid and plastic waste treatment — To enhance recycling waste and contribute to reduction of ocean plastics

JCM = Joint Crediting Mechanism, SDG = Sustainable Development Goal.

only assists them in relation to the JCM approval process, but can also support a company's internal communication and decision-making process, particularly in aligning their business strategies to SDGs.

JCM partner countries can likewise benefit from the linkage guidance, from assisting them in prioritizing certain goals and targets, to better understanding the SD attribute of projects they are asked to approve.

Source: T. Murun and A. Tsukui. 2020. *Joint Crediting Mechanism and Sustainable Development Goals Linkage Guidance*. Hayama: Institute for Global Environmental Strategies.

---

[23] T. Murun and A. Tsukui. 2020. *Joint Crediting Mechanism Contributions to Sustainable Development Goals*. Tokyo: Ministry of the Environment, Government of Japan.

4.5 Avoidance of Double Counting

The Japan-Indonesia bilateral agreement for the JCM has a specific provision for both sides to ensure avoidance of double counting by not using projects for purposes of "other international climate mitigation mechanisms."

In terms of JCM accounting, Indonesia has two registry systems:

(i) the JCM Registry that records the emission reduction achieved by the JCM project and the portioning of those credits (Figure 14),[24] and

(ii) the National Registry System (SRN) on Climate Change Control that records both the net emission level (for national inventory purposes) and the emission reduction (Figure 15).[25]

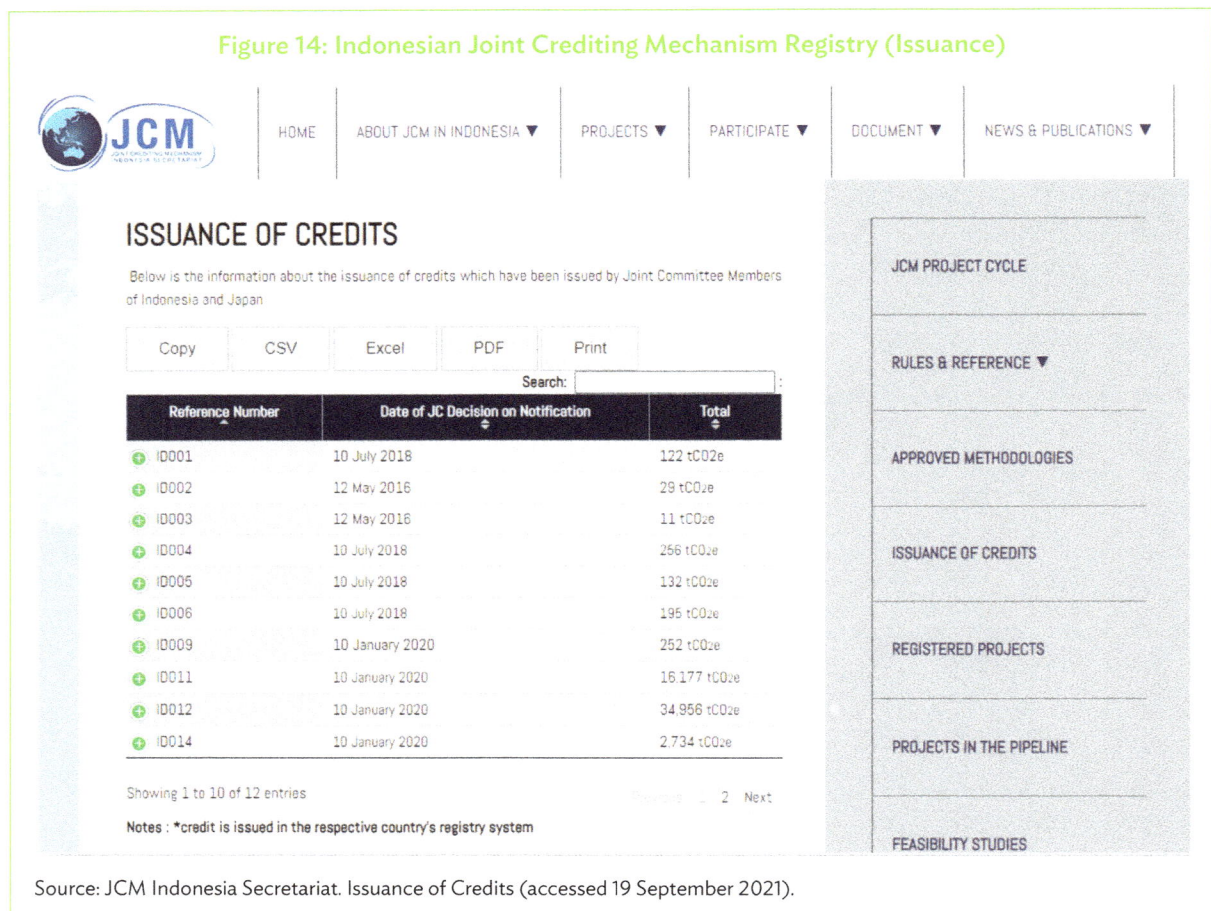

Figure 14: Indonesian Joint Crediting Mechanism Registry (Issuance)

Source: JCM Indonesia Secretariat. Issuance of Credits (accessed 19 September 2021).

---

[24] JCM Indonesia Secretariat. Issuance of Credits (accessed 19 September 2021).
[25] National Registry System on Climate Change Control.

Figure 15: National Registry System on Climate Change Control Registry

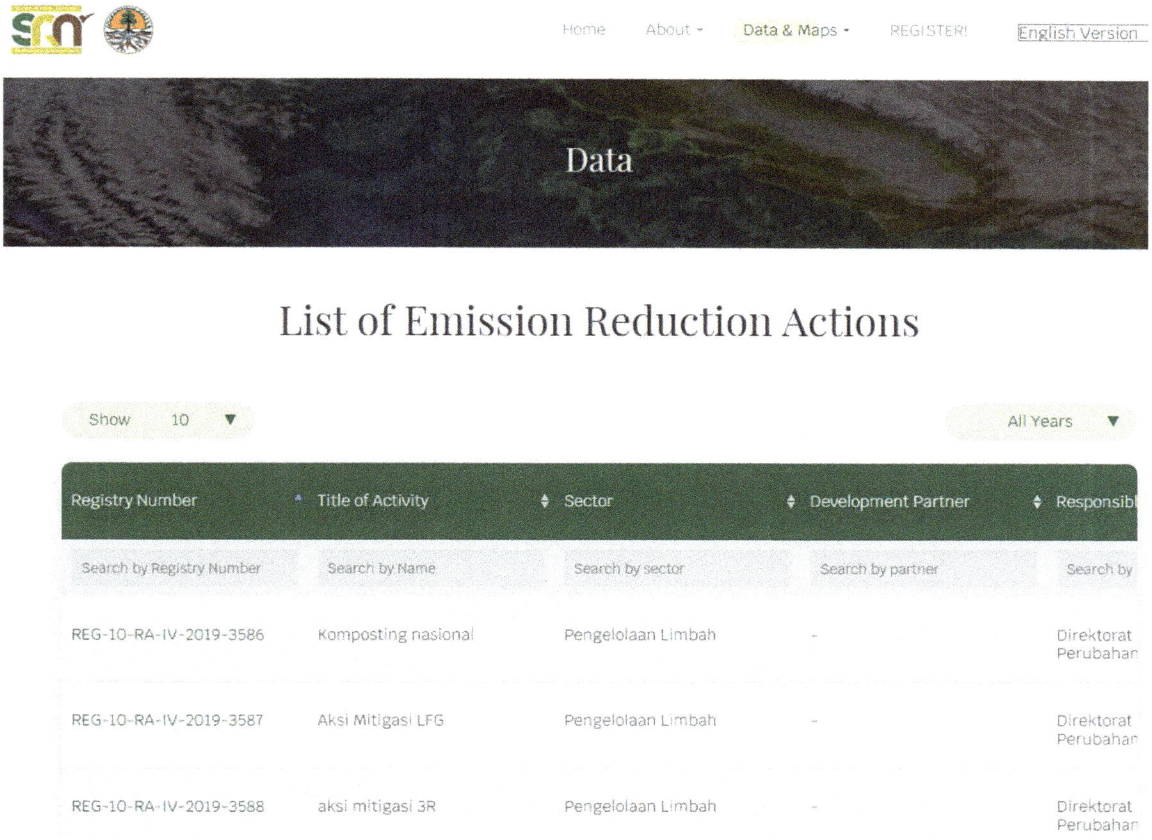

Source: National Registry System on Climate Change Control. GHG Emissions Reduction Action Data (accessed 24 September 2021).

The two are already linked in the sense that the JCM Secretariat will input project information into the SRN registry. The JCM Secretariat also provides the breakdown of JCM credits according to ownership when reporting to the SRN.

At the national level, Indonesia has multiple active advanced registry systems (Figure 16). It is therefore in a strong position to fully digitally integrate the JCM registry and SRN registry, which in turn can link to the national inventory. However, digital integration/reconciliation between the JCM registry and SRN is not expected to be established in the immediate future due to the complexity of integrating cross-ministerial registries.

Figure 16: Indonesian Joint Crediting Mechanism Registries

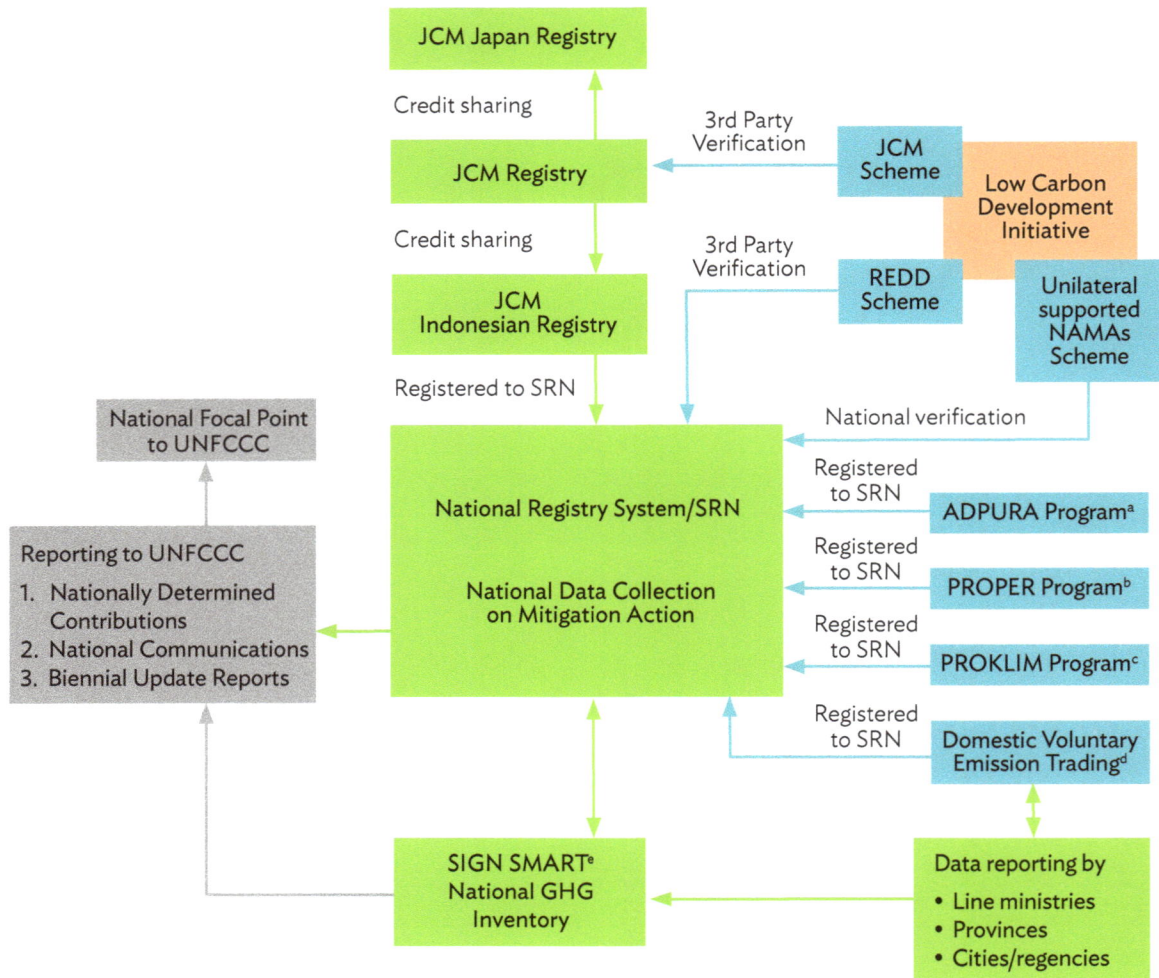

GHG = greenhouse gas; JCM = Joint Crediting Mechanism; PROPER = Pollution Control, Evaluation, and Rating; REDD = Reducing Emissions from Deforestation and Forest Degradation in Developing Countries; NAMA = Nationally Appropriate Mitigation Action; SRN = National Registry System on Climate Change Control; UNFCCC = United Nations Framework Convention on Climate Change.

Notes:
a   The ADIPURA Program is a national clean cities program aimed at realizing sustainable cities through a regional approach, through for example evaluating of waste management practices.
b   The PROPER Program is a national level public evaluation and reporting program aimed at promoting industrial compliance with pollution control regulations.
c   The Climate Village Program (ProKlim) is a national program aimed at increasing the active participation of local communities in implementing climate change mitigation and adaptation actions.
d   Voluntary emission trading schemes include one currently being piloted for coal-fired power plants through the dedicated electronic platform APPLE GATRIK, as well as ones in the pipeline such as the Indonesia Certified Emission Reduction for which public consultations have been held.
e   SIGN SMART is the web-based inventory designed to support national (line ministries) and sub-national GHG inventory activities.

Source: Adapted by ADB using information from the JCM Secretariat.

4.6 Reporting

The discussion here again will not go into the specifics of the prerequisites for Article 6.2 at the national level that is not under the purview of nor directly related to the JCM.

With regard to the relationship between the ITMOs and the corresponding adjustment to the national inventory for the NDC, Indonesia adopts a single-year target, with an unconditional target of 29% and a conditional target of up to 41% of the BAU scenario by 2030.[26]

For the sake of simplicity, Indonesia may consider using the average annual amount of ITMOs first transferred and apply it once to the NDC, in 2030. It should be pointed out that a Party (Indonesia) must adhere to its chosen method consistently throughout the NDC implementation period.

---

[26] Government of Indonesia. 2021. *Updated Nationally Determined Contribution*. Jakarta.

5 Project-Level Analysis

A project-level analysis in relation to Article 6.2 alignment has been carried out using one implemented JCM project from Indonesia: JCM_ID011 Reduction of Energy Consumption by Introducing an Energy-Efficient Waste Paper Processing System into a Packaging Paper Factory in Bekasi, West Java ("the Bekasi Project"). The project was selected due to its having been registered and implemented under JCM rules and having had one of the largest volumes of issued JCM credits to date.

The project, with an expected operational lifetime of 12 years, was registered as a JCM project to conduct MRV between 2017 and 2020. The JCM credits from this period are estimated as 71,291 tCO_2 in total, with 16,177 tCO_2 of this already verified and issued.

While the project has already been completed prior to the Paris Agreement era, the analysis will attempt to theoretically and retroactively align the project procedures to Article 6.2 to draw out the lessons learned that could be transferred to meaningful action for 2021 and beyond.

As identified in Section 2.1, the following six elements are to be ensured in projects under the cooperative approach:

(i) Real and verified emission reductions
(ii) Additional emission reductions
(iii) Authorization
(iv) Sustainable development
(v) Avoidance of double counting
(vi) Reporting

These will be discussed in the Bekasi Project's context in Section 5.3.

5.1 Introduction of the Case Study

Indonesia's high economic growth has driven demand for paper, including cardboard. PT Fajar Surya Wisesa owns and operates an expanding packaging paper factory in Bekasi, West Java, that hosts the JCM project.

As per the JCM project design document, the production of corrugated carton mainly involves two processes: old corrugated cartons (OCC) process and sheet forming process. The JCM project will introduce energy efficiency technologies from Aikawa Iron Works in the OCC process of its newly built production line.[27] Figure 17 shows the CO_2 reductions in the OCC process.

The project was supported by the Ministry of the Environment, Japan (MOEJ) through the Financing Program for JCM Model Projects.

---

[27] Kanematsu Corp. 2017. JCM Project Design Document Form.

Figure 17: Carbon Dioxide Reductions in Old Corrugated Cartons Process of Cardboard Production

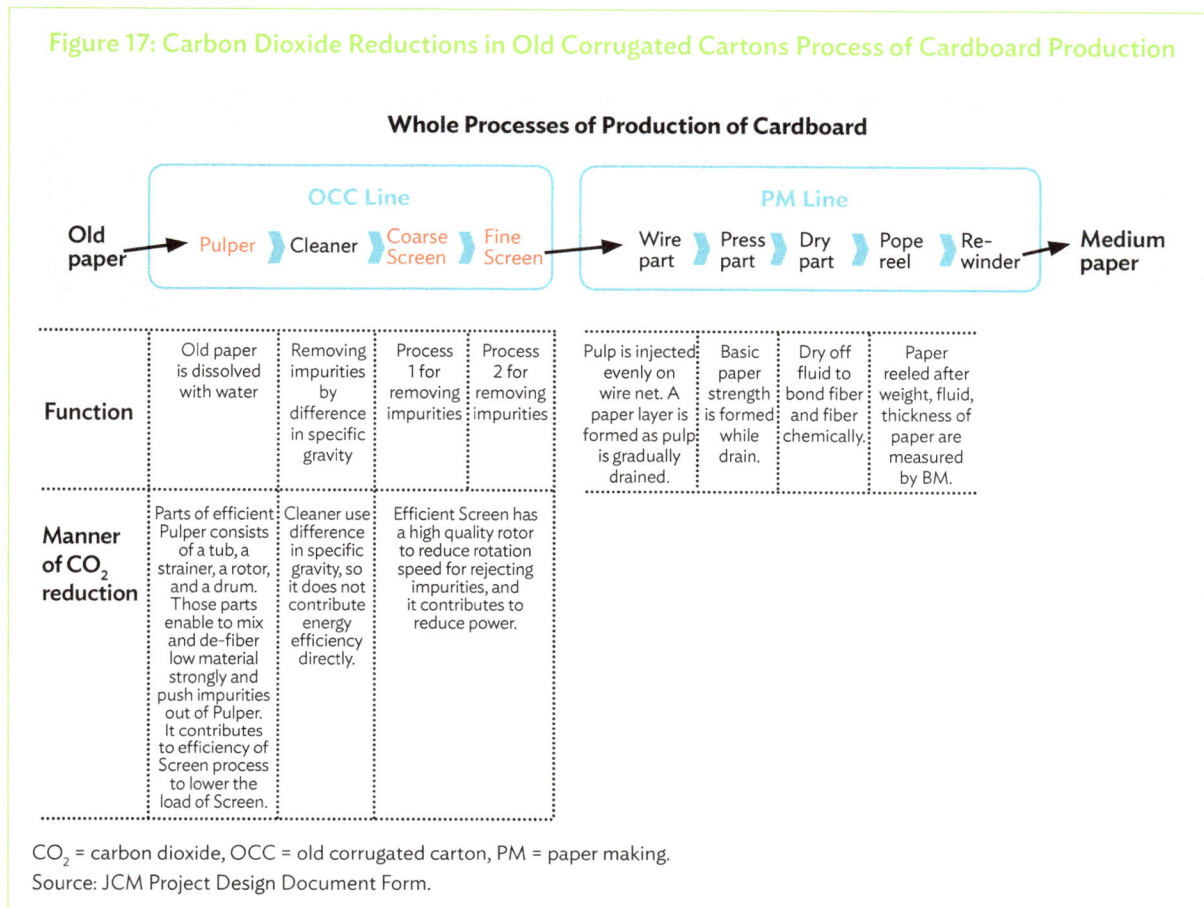

Whole Processes of Production of Cardboard

Old paper → [OCC Line: Pulper › Cleaner › Coarse Screen › Fine Screen] → [PM Line: Wire part › Press part › Dry part › Pope reel › Re-winder] → Medium paper

Function	Old paper is dissolved with water	Removing impurities by difference in specific gravity	Process 1 for removing impurities	Process 2 for removing impurities	Pulp is injected evenly on wire net. A paper layer is formed as pulp is gradually drained.	Basic paper strength is formed while drain.	Dry off fluid to bond fiber and fiber chemically.	Paper reeled after weight, fluid, thickness of paper are measured by BM.
Manner of CO$_2$ reduction	Parts of efficient Pulper consists of a tub, a strainer, a rotor, and a drum. Those parts enable to mix and de-fiber low material strongly and push impurities out of Pulper. It contributes to efficiency of Screen process to lower the load of Screen.	Cleaner use difference in specific gravity, so it does not contribute energy efficiency directly.	Efficient Screen has a high quality rotor to reduce rotation speed for rejecting impurities, and it contributes to reduce power.					

CO$_2$ = carbon dioxide, OCC = old corrugated carton, PM = paper making.
Source: JCM Project Design Document Form.

5.2 How the Case Study Project Aligns with Article 6.2 Requirements

5.2.1 Real and Verified Emission Reductions

The project used the approved JCM methodology ID_AM012 Ver1.0: Reduction of Energy Consumption by Introducing an Energy-Efficient Old Corrugated Carton Processing System into a Cardboard Factory to calculate emission reductions.[28]

Reference emissions are calculated based on the unit electricity consumption of the reference (existing) OCC line (MWh per ton of paper production), the paper production level of the project OCC line (ton of paper production), and the grid emission factor of electricity (tCO$_2$e per MWh). Project emissions are calculated based on the electricity consumption of the project OCC line (ton of paper production) and the grid emission factor of electricity.

The emission reductions are calculated as the difference between reference emissions and project emissions.

[28] JCM Indonesia Secretariat. ID_AM012—Reduction of Energy Consumption by Introducing an Energy-Efficient Old Corrugated Carton Processing System into a Cardboard Factory.

Of the input values, two parameters were fixed *ex ante*: the unit electricity consumption of the reference (existing) OCC line that is calculated based on actual historical electricity consumption of the existing OCC line, and the grid emission factor of electricity. That these parameters are fixed *ex ante* after having been validated by the TPE is comparable to CDM and Gold Standard methods and appropriate.

Other values, namely the electricity consumption and production level of the project OCC line were monitored *ex post* and verified by the TPE for the period of 1 July 2017 to 31 August 2018, resulting in verified emission reductions of 16,177 tCO_2 for the said period.

Emission reductions have been duly verified at the project level.

5.2.2 Additional Emission Reductions

The quantification of additional emission reductions is dependent on the reference emission level that is set by the approved JCM methodology ID_AM012 Ver1.0. According to the methodology, the reference emissions are calculated conservatively based on the past performance by averaging the values of the specific electricity consumption without those that exceed two times the standard deviation above the mean within 2 years from the timing of validation of the existing OCC lines of the same factory where the project OCC line(s) is installed. This can be interpreted that the reference emission level is the continuation of current practice, calculated conservatively. The difference between this reference emission level and emissions achieved below it is considered additional emission reductions.

The Bekasi Project's crediting period has ended in 2020, prior to the Paris Agreement era. Therefore, naturally, the methodology's reference emission level discussions do not explicitly consider Indonesia's NDC targets. If the Bekasi Project were to instead have been implemented under Article 6.2, the methodology would be considered to be not aligned with Article 6.2 as it does not consider Indonesia's NDC.

5.2.3 Authorization

The Bekasi Project has been through two approvals. The first was for the approval of the activity as a JCM project. The project was accepted by the Joint Committee and registered on 22 December 2017.

The second approval, and the one which would be equivalent to the authorization under Article 6.2, was for the issuance of the JCM credits for its first monitoring period of 1 July 2017 to 31 August 2018. The issuance for the Bekasi Project's JCM credits for this period was approved by the Joint Committee on 10 January 2020.

Being implemented before the Paris Agreement, the approval process did not involve issues that will be pertinent to future authorizations, such as those relating to the effect on Indonesia's NDC.

5.2.4 Sustainable Development

Completion and submission of the SDIP and SDIR at validation and verification, respectively, is a prerequisite under the JCM rules of Indonesia.

For the Bekasi Project, the SDIP was submitted together with the comprehensive UKL–UPL that was approved by the Environmental Management Agency of Bekasi Regency. The submitted SDIP has not been disclosed on the JCM public website, while the approved UKL–UPL has been; therefore, UKL–UPL is analyzed under this section. The UKL–UPL relates to the JCM project and to a limited extent the entire Fajar factory, and assesses the social and environmental impact during construction and operation, including

(i)   the quality of soil/groundwater in connection to the wastewater generated,
(ii)   stormwater runoff,
(iii)   ambient air quality,
(iv)   noise,
(v)   job opportunity,
(vi)   safety and health,
(vii)   security, and
(viii) traffic.

Positive impacts included a decrease in the amount of waste generation expected and prioritizing additional local hiring.

Although not a part of the official JCM project cycle, the Bekasi Project was additionally studied in the aforementioned Institute for Global Environmental Strategies JCM-SDG Linkage Guidance, which summarizes the project's attributes in Table 7.

The SDIR has been submitted as part of the verification process as an *ex post* evaluation of the contribution to sustainable development as outlined in the *ex ante* SDIP.

The SDIP was submitted but not uploaded on the JCM website.

Table 7: Sustainable Development Attributes of the Bekasi Project

Waste recycling related projects Reduction of Energy Consumption by Introducing an Energy-Efficient Waste Paper Processing System into a Packaging Paper Factory		
SDG Target	**Indicator**	**Project's contribution to the SDGs**
8.2	Achieving higher levels of economic productivity through diversification, technological upgrading and innovation, including through a focus on high-value added and labor-intensive sectors	Helping to upgrade technology in factories in developing countries
12.2	By 2030, achieve the sustainable management and efficient use of natural resources	Recycling materials
12.4	By 2020, achieve the environmentally sound management of chemicals and all wastes throughout their life cycle, in accordance with agreed international frameworks, and significantly reduce their release to air, water and soil in order to minimize their adverse impacts on human health and the environment	CO_2 emission reduction (Unit: tCO_2e)
		Issued credits based on tracking and reporting the amount of GHG emission reductions (Unit: tons)

GHG = greenhouse gas, SDG = Sustainable Development Goal, tCO_2e = tons of carbon dioxide equivalent.
Source: T. Murun and A. Tsukui. 2020. *Joint Crediting Mechanism Contributions to Sustainable Development Goals.* Tokyo: Ministry of the Environment, Government of Japan.

5.2.5　Avoidance of Double Counting

Of the 16,177 tCO$_2$ JCM credits issued for the Bekasi Project on 10 January 2020, the issuance of the credits for Indonesia (7,441 tCO$_2$) occurred on 15 January 2020 with the unique identifiers: JCM-ID-011-03-01-ID-0000296 - JCM-ID-011-03-01-ID-0007736. Similarly, the issuance of the credits for Japan (8,736 tCO$_2$) occurred on 16 January 2020 with the unique identifiers: JCM-ID-JP-582-9317-01101.

As per Figures 15–16, this information is then to be registered with the SRN. However, the Bekasi Project data is not yet reflected in the SRN. According to the JCM Secretariat, this is due to an onsite visit by the SRN Secretarial Team to validate the activity for its purposes (separate to the verification process for emission reductions) not yet having occurred.

Due to the unavailability of data for the Bekasi Project, for this section the JCM project JCM_ID002, which is to date the only JCM project whose data are reflected in the SRN, was studied.

In the same manner as the Bekasi Project, a total of 29 tCO$_2$ credits were issued for the project JCM_ID002, with 6 issued to Indonesia and 23 issued to Japan. These are duly reflected in the JCM registry as can be seen in Figure 18. A separate page shows a further breakdown of: 3 credits to the Indonesian project participant, 3 credits to the Japanese project participant, 3 credits to the Government of Indonesia and 20 credits to the Government of Japan. The JCM Secretariat has also registered the project under the SRN, reporting both the total emission reduction (29 tCO$_2$) as well as the breakdown of credits belonging to each stakeholder as shown on Figure 18.

Figure 18: Joint Crediting Mechanism Registry Data for Project JCM_ID002

Issuance request state	Verification report
	SDIR
	Notified
	Date of JC decision on notification: 12 May 16
	Total amount of credits to be issued: 29
	(Indonesia)
	Notified amount of credits to be issued: 6
	JCM-ID-002-03-01-ID-0000001-JCM-ID-002-03-01-ID-0000006
	(Japan)
	Notified amount of credits to be issued: 23
	JCM-ID-JP-1-23-00201

Note: This is what the public sees upon checking the project details on the JCM Indonesia Secretariat's website.
Source: JCM Indonesia Secretariat. Issuance of Credits (accessed 19 September 2021).

The SRN registry for JCM_ID002 at a glance shows only the total emission reductions for the entire project, giving a puzzling first impression (Figure 19).

However, further into the registry, the "After Mitigation Emission" (total net emissions from the JCM project facility) is reported (Figure 20). It is this figure, rather than the emission reductions, that is fed into the national inventory.

Figure 19: National Registry System on Climate Change Control Data for Project JCM_ID002 (1)

Show 10 ▼ All Years ▼

Registry Number	Title of Activity	Sector	Development Partner	Responsible Parties	Institut
Search by Registry Number	Search by Name	Search by sector	Search by partner	sekretariat JCM indonesia	Search
REG-11-PR-XII-2016-0463	Project of Introducing High Efficiency Refrigerator to a Food Industry Cold Storage in Indonesia	Energi	1. Mayekawa MFG Co. Ltd (Bekasi, provinsi Jawa Barat)	Sekretariat JCM Indonesia	Kement

Responsible Parties	Institution	Scheme/Actor	Emission Reduction Claimed (1000 TON CO2E/Year)	Verified Emission Reduction (1000 TON CO2E/Year)
sekretariat JCM indonesia	Search by Institution	Search by scheme	Search by ER Claimed	Search by ER Verified
Sekretariat JCM Indonesia	Kementerian/Lembaga	Dunia Usaha	• 2015 - 0.029	-

Source: National Registry System on Climate Change Control. GHG Emissions Production Action Data (accessed 24 September 2021).

Figure 20: National Registry System on Climate Change Control Data for Project JCM_ID002 (2)

Action

Category of Action
Mitigasi

Scheme/Actor
Dunia Usaha

Field/Sector
Dunia Usaha

Related program
-

Reporting year
Feb-2015 s/d Jul-2015

Baseline emission (thousand tones CO_2e / year)
-

After Mitigation Emission (thousand tones CO_2e / year)

- 2015 : 0.102

Reduction emission claimed (thousand tones CO_2e / year)

- 2015 : 0.029

Verified reduction emission (thousand tones CO_2e / year)
-

Source: National Registry System on Climate Change Control. Activity Details (accessed 24 September 2021).

The JCM and SRN registry systems are in full alignment for purposes of Article 6.2, on the assumption that the SRN validation visits are conducted, and its results reflected prior to official updates to the national inventory. Further institutional provisions for applying corresponding adjustments are necessary as discussed in Section 3.1.5.

Naturally, corresponding adjustments have not been applied to JCM projects that have issued credits only up to 31 December 2020, including the Bekasi Project and project JCM_ID002.

5.2.6 Reporting

Reporting at the project level was only conducted with the Joint Committee through the JCM Secretariat. No deficiencies were identified at the project level.

6 Analysis

In the previous sections, alignment of the JCM with Article 6.2 was analyzed at the main framework level, national level, and project level. This section summarizes the key steps and processes that JCM projects have already achieved, and status of alignment with A6.2.[29] Two sets of analyses are presented below. The first looks at the alignment from the perspective of fulfilling elements under Article 6.2 (Table 8). The second looks at the alignment from the perspective of the JCM project cycle (Table 9). Although there is an overlap between the two, they are meant to help different stakeholders—whether policy makers or project participants—understand the JCM and Article 6.2 alignment.

Table 8: Status of Joint Crediting Mechanism Alignment to Elements under Article 6.2

Elements under A6.2	Current Status of Alignment	Remarks
Sustainable development	Fully aligned	N/A
Real and verified emission reductions	Fully aligned	N/A
Additional emission reductions	Not aligned	This will be a unique feature within Article 6.2 to consider NDC ambitions to ensure that they result in additional emission reductions.
Authorization	Partially aligned	The JCM approval process operates under the JCM bilateral agreements and includes explicitly seeking approvals from both countries. However, the agreements were drawn up prior to the Paris Agreement and do not refer explicitly to authorizations as defined by Article 6.2.
Avoidance of double counting	Partially aligned	While the inherent mechanics remain the same, host countries will select the mode of corresponding adjustment (single/multi-year).
Reporting	Partially aligned	While host countries have gained experience in reporting, Article 6.2 would require establishment of data flow of JCM credit issuance results to partner country NDC.

JCM = Joint Crediting Mechanism, N/A = not applicable, NDC = nationally determined contribution.
Source: Asian Development Bank.

Of the six elements identified, the four that require action to varying degrees include sustainable development, additional emission reductions or "additionality," authorization, and avoidance of double counting. These may not be required just under A6.2 but also under bilateral mechanisms more broadly under the Paris Agreement. Regardless of these open issues that host countries will need to work on, they can still build on their existing experiences from the JCM, as such are covered to a certain degree. The key is to understand, in the national and project level circumstances, what are things that can be carried from the JCM and what are things that need additional effort to be eligible under Article 6.2. Table 9 below complements and demonstrates this finding through detailed analysis in the project level.

---

[29] The details of the JCM project process is summarized in the Article 6 of the Paris Agreement: Drawing Lessons from the Joint Crediting Mechanism. ADB. 2019. *Article 6 of the Paris Agreement: Drawing Lessons from the Joint Crediting Mechanism*. Manila.

Table 9: Joint Crediting Mechanism Project Cycle and Alignment to Elements under Article 6.2

Joint Crediting Mechanism Steps	Article 6.2 Relevant Elements	Level of Intervention and Approach Taken	Current Status of Alignment	Remarks
Methodology Development and Approval	Real and verified emission reductions	Project Level Joint Crediting Mechanism (JCM) methodology ID_ AM012 Ver1.0 was developed and require historical data and monitoring of key parameters.	Fully aligned	N/A
	Additional emission reductions	Framework and National Level In the methodology, the reference emissions were set conservatively based on past performance.	Partially aligned	Experience of developing methodologies and conservative approach taken by the JCM would allow countries to adjust protocols for new methodologies that would consider national circumstances and nationally determined contribution (NDC) ambitions of the host country to ensure they result in additional emission reductions.
	Methodology approval	National Level Methodology was submitted to and approved by the Joint Committee.	Fully aligned	The approach of having methodologies approved at the partner country level allows national circumstances to be taken into account, and is in tune with the need to align future methodologies to individual country NDC ambitions.
Project Design Document Development	Sustainable development	National Level Indonesia requires the submission of a Sustainable Development Implementation Plan (SDIP). SDIP was prepared and submitted to TPE.	Fully aligned	N/A
	Real and verified emission reductions	Project Level Historical data were used for parameters fixed ex ante. Estimates of operational data were used for parameters to be monitored ex post. Calculations were carried out in accordance with the approved JCM methodology.	Fully aligned	N/A
	Additional emission reductions	Framework and National Level The reference emissions were calculated conservatively using historical data in accordance with the approved JCM methodology.	Not aligned	Use of methodologies that were developed considering national circumstance and NDC ambition would allow projects to result in additional emission reductions.

continued on next page

Table 9 *continued*

Joint Crediting Mechanism Steps	Article 6.2 Relevant Elements	Level of Intervention and Approach Taken	Current Status of Alignment	Remarks
Validation	Real and verified emission reductions	Project Level Third-party entity (TPE) validated the values indicated in the Project Design Document.	Fully aligned	N/A
Registration	Authorization (for participation)	Framework and National Level The project was accepted by the Joint Committee and registered.	Partially aligned	JCM bilateral agreements were drawn up prior to the Paris Agreement and do not refer explicitly to authorizations as defined by Article 6.2.
Monitoring	Real and verified emission reductions	Project Level Project participants monitored the required monitoring parameters in accordance with the approved JCM methodology.	Fully aligned	N/A
Verification	Sustainable development	National Level Indonesia requires the submission of a Sustainable Development Implementation Report (SDIR). SDIR was prepared and submitted to TPE.	Fully aligned	N/A
	Real and verified emission reductions	Framework and National Level TPE verified the monitored data.	Fully aligned	N/A
Issuance of Credits	Authorization (for internationally transferred mitigation outcomes)	Framework and National Level Credits from the first monitoring period were issued.	Partially aligned	JCM bilateral agreements were drawn up prior to the Paris Agreement and do not refer explicitly to authorizations as defined by Article 6.2 and explore optimal procedure for authorizing internationally transferred mitigation outcomes of other mechanisms.
	Reporting	Framework and National Level Reporting of the credit issuance to the Japanese and Indonesian JCM registries was conducted with the Joint Committee through the JCM Secretariat.	Partially aligned	While host countries have gained experience in reporting, Article 6.2 would require establishment of data flow of JCM credit issuance results to partner country NDC.

continued on next page

Table 9   *continued*

Joint Crediting Mechanism Steps	Article 6.2 Relevant Elements	Level of Intervention and Approach Taken	Current Status of Alignment	Remarks
	Avoidance of double counting	<u>Framework Level</u> The JCM Registry places unique identifiers on issued credits, which were apportioned to the respective project participants and governments. <u>National Level</u> On the Indonesian side, the National Registry System on Climate Change Control (SRN) records both the net emission level (for national inventory purposes) and the emission reduction. The data for the Bekasi Project has been duly submitted and is awaiting a validation team visit by the SRN Secretariat for it to be reflected in the SRN system.	Partially aligned	While the inherent mechanics remain the same, host countries will select the mode of corresponding adjustment (single/multi-year).

JCM = Joint Crediting Mechanism, N/A = not applicable, NDC = nationally determined contribution, SDIP = Sustainable Development Implementation Plan, SDIR = Sustainable Development Implementation Report, TPE = third-party entity.

Source: Asian Development Bank.

7 Conclusion

The analysis from this publication highlights that the JCM can indeed be regarded as a forerunner for operationalization of Article 6.2, both from the perspective of Article 6.2 being decentralized, and that the JCM framework is already very closely aligned with what is required, having been specifically conceived with future international agreements in mind.

With only a few practical modifications and with no fundamental change required, the 17 countries that already have bilateral agreements on the JCM with the Government of Japan, have an early mover advantage in operationalizing Article 6.2 of the Paris Agreement.

The strength of the JCM is not only in its general alignment to Article 6.2—an understanding that was reinforced by the multi-level analysis conducted in this paper. It is also that the JCM is an already established and fully operational bilateral mechanism that puts it in a perfect position for countries to use to take specific and concrete action. The few gaps identified and in need of action are indeed best rectified through targeted bilateral discussion that allows consideration of varying national circumstances and offers flexibility and opportunity to learn by doing.

This comparative analysis has enhanced the knowledge on how bilateral approaches can be implemented under Article 6 of the Paris Agreement and provides insights to future development of similar bilateral crediting mechanisms. In addition, alongside providing important insights to JCM host countries on how their engagement with the JCM has enabled to build a significant capacity to potentially operationalize Article 6.2, the publication is also helpful to countries that are yet to participate under the JCM to understand the considerations and opportunities in doing so with respect to Article 6.2 moving forward and building synergies accordingly.

APPENDIX 1

Approved Japan Fund for the Joint Crediting Mechanism Projects

No.	Project	Country	JFJCM grant	Approval	Estimated annual emission reductions	Technologies supported
1	Preparing Outer Islands for Sustainable Energy Development Project (POISED)	Maldives	$5 million	Mar 2015	1,300 tCO$_2$e	Advanced battery system and energy management system (EMS)
2	Southwest Transmission Grid Expansion Project	Bangladesh	$7 million	Jul 2018	23,100 tCO$_2$e	Energy-efficient transmission lines
3	Upscaling Renewable Energy Sector Project	Mongolia	$6 million	Sep 2018	6,400 tCO$_2$e	Solar photovoltaic with advanced battery system and EMS
4	Improving Access to Health Services for Disadvantaged Groups Investment Program	Mongolia	$3.48 million	Oct 2019	2,900 tCO$_2$e	Energy-efficient HVAC, high insulation window, rooftop solar photovoltaic and ground source heat pump
5	Greater Malé Waste to Energy Project	Maldives	$10 million	Aug 2020	40,400 tCO$_2$e (average for 20 years)	Waste to energy plant (incineration)

HVAC = heating, ventilation, and air conditioning; JFJCM = Japan Fund for the Joint Crediting Mechanism.
Source: Asian Development Bank.

Joint Crediting Mechanism
Approved Methodology

Joint Crediting Mechanism Approved Methodology ID_AM012
"Reduction of Energy Consumption by Introducing an Energy-Efficient Old Corrugated
Carton Processing System into a Cardboard Factory"

A. Title of the methodology

Reduction of Energy Consumption by Introducing an Energy-Efficient Old Corrugated Carton Processing System into a Cardboard Factory, Version 1.0

B. Terms and definitions

Terms	Definitions
Old Corrugated Carton Line (OCC line)	A process for adjusting materials to be delivered to the following paper making line (PM line) in the corrugated carton production process. The energy used by the OCC line is electricity. It mainly consists of a pulper which melts old corrugated carton and a screen which refines the corrugated medium, and also motor, pump, agitator, thickener, and cleaner.
Paper Machine Line (PM line)	A process for making paper in a corrugated carton production process.
Paper Yield	Percentage of paper production output in the recycled paper input to the OCC line.

C. Summary of the methodology

Items	Summary
GHG emission reduction measures	This methodology targets introduction of energy saving technologies, i.e. energy-efficient old corrugated carton processing system, to OCC lines in a cardboard factory. Mechanical efficiency of each element device is improved and system configuration and control are optimized in the energy-efficient old corrugated carton processing system, e.g. improvement of impeller-shape in an agitator leading to higher

JCM_ID_AM012_ver01.0
Sectoral scopes: 03 and 04

	motor efficiency and optimization of the system configuration of pumps, which leads to a reduction of the electricity consumptions, and consequently GHG emission reductions.
Calculation of reference emissions	Reference emissions are calculated from the energy intensity (specific energy consumption) of the reference OCC line(s), the project paper production and the emission factor for consumed electricity.
Calculation of project emissions	Project emissions are calculated from the electricity consumption by the project OCC line and the emission factor for consumed electricity.
Monitoring parameters	• Paper production measured at the PM line connected to the project OCC line • Electricity consumption of the project OCC line

D. Eligibility criteria

This methodology is applicable to projects that satisfy all of the following criteria.

Criterion 1	The specific energy consumption of the project OCC line guaranteed by the manufacture is, at the minimum, less than the reference specific energy consumption set for the project factory.
Criterion 2	The paper yield of the project OCC line(s) guaranteed by the manufacture is equal to or more than 90% at the range of designed production capacity.
Criterion 3	Production capacity of the project OCC line is no more than the twice as large as the capacity of the existing OCC line.
Criterion 4	Plan for regular adjustment, replacement, and improvements of project OCC line(s) is prepared (at least once every six months).

E. Emission Sources and GHG types

Reference emissions	
Emission sources	**GHG types**
Electricity consumption by the reference OCC line(s)	CO_2
Project emissions	
Emission sources	**GHG types**

2

JCM_ID_AM012_ver01.0
Sectoral scopes: 03 and 04

Electricity consumption by the project OCC line(s)	CO_2

F. Establishment and calculation of reference emissions

F.1. Establishment of reference emissions

In this methodology, the reference emissions are calculated conservatively based on the past performance by averaging the values of the specific electricity consumption (SEC) without those which exceed 2 times the standard deviation above the mean within two years from the timing of validation of the existing OCC lines of the same factory where the project OCC line(s) is installed.

Net emission reductions are achieved by fixing the default value of specific electricity consumption (i.e. amount of electricity consumed by the OCC line to produce one unit of paper product measured at the PM line) of the reference OCC line conservatively in the following manner:

- Collect 300 data sets of daily electricity consumption by the OCC line* and daily volume of paper product at the PM line connected to the OCC line and calculate the SEC of the OCC line for each daily data by dividing electricity consumption by volume of paper product.
  *Electricity consumption by the OCC line can be measured with a measuring equipment or can be estimated from measured electricity consumption of the whole corrugated carton production process consisting of the OCC line and the PM line based on the ratio of the rated power consumption in each line.
- Calculate the reference specific energy consumption (SEC_{RE}) by averaging the values of the SEC without those which exceed 2 times the standard deviation above the mean.
- Where multiple OCC lines exist in the factory, select the most recently installed OCC line(s) for data collection.
- Where recently more than one OCC line installed (at the same time), select one with the highest efficiency as the reference OCC line.
- If the existing OCC line has been installed as a JCM project, data of such OCC line is excluded from calculation of the default value.

F.2. Calculation of reference emissions

3

JCM_ID_AM012_ver01.0
Sectoral scopes: 03 and 04

$$RE_p = \sum_j \left(EC_{RE,j,p} \times EF_{elec} \right)$$

$$EC_{RE,j,p} = SEC_{RE} \times PP_{j,p}$$

Where

RE_p	:	Reference emissions during the period p [tCO$_2$/p]
$EC_{RE,j,p}$	:	Electricity consumption by the reference OCC line j during the period p [MWh/p]
EF_{elec}	:	CO$_2$ emission factor for consumed electricity [tCO$_2$/MWh]
SEC_{RE}	:	Reference specific electricity consumption of the OCC line [MWh/ton]
$PP_{j,p}$	:	Paper production measured at the PM line connected to the project OCC line j during the period p [ton/p]
j	:	Identification number of the OCC line

G. Calculation of project emissions

$$PE_p = \sum_j \left(EC_{PJ,j,p} \times EF_{elec} \right)$$

Where

PE_p	:	Project emissions during the period p [tCO$_2$/p]
$EC_{PJ,j,p}$	:	Electricity consumption by the project OCC line j during the period p [MWh/p]
EF_{elec}	:	CO$_2$ emission factor for consumed electricity [tCO$_2$/MWh]
j	:	Identification number of the OCC line

H. Calculation of emissions reductions

$$ER_p = RE_p - PE_p$$

Where

4

ER_p	: Emission reductions during the period p [tCO$_2$/p]
RE_p	: Reference emissions during the period p [tCO$_2$/p]
PE_p	: Project emissions during the period p [tCO$_2$/p]

I. Data and parameters fixed *ex ante*

The source of each data and parameter fixed *ex ante* is listed as below.

Parameter	Description of data	Source
SEC_{RE}	Reference specific electricity consumption of the OCC line [MWh/ton] The value for each project is fixed ex ante by the project participant in line with the procedures described in the section F.1 in this methodology.	Data of daily electricity consumption by the OCC line and daily volume of paper product at the PM line connected to the OCC line within two years from the timing of validation of the existing OCC lines of the same factory where the project OCC line(s) is installed.
EF_{elec}	CO$_2$ emission factor for consumed electricity [tCO$_2$/MWh]. When the project equipment consumes only grid electricity or captive electricity, the project participant applies the CO$_2$ emission factor respectively. When the project equipment may consume both grid electricity and captive electricity, the project participant applies the CO$_2$ emission factors for grid ($EF_{elec,gr}$) and captive ($EF_{elec,ca}$) electricity proportionately. Where multiple fuel types are consumed as captive power sources, the emission factor ($EF_{elec,ca,i}$) and proportion of ($\propto_i$) each fuel type i is identified and applied.	[Grid electricity] The data is sourced from "Emission Factors of Electricity Interconnection Systems", National Committee on Clean Development Mechanism (Indonesian DNA for CDM), based on data obtained by Directorate General of Electricity, Ministry of Energy and Mineral Resources, Indonesia, unless otherwise instructed by the Joint Committee. [Captive electricity] Specification of the captive power generation system including co-generation system provided by

$$EF_{elec} = \left(EF_{elec,gr} \times \alpha_{gr}\right) + \sum_i \left(EF_{elec,ca,i} \times \alpha_i\right)$$

Where:

α_{gr}: Proportion of grid electricity to the total electricity consumed [fraction]

Proportion of captive electricity generated with a specific fuel type i is derived from dividing captive electricity generated with a specific fuel type i ($EG_{gen,i,p}$)* by total electricity consumed at the project site. The total electricity consumed is a summation of grid electricity imported ($EI_{grid,p}$) and total captive electricity generated at the project site ($EG_{gen,total,p}$) during the monitoring period.

$$\alpha_i = \frac{EG_{gen,i,p}}{EI_{grid,p} + EG_{gen,total,p}}$$

* Captive electricity generated is measured with measuring equipment such as electric power meter which is certified in compliance with national/international standards. In case a calibration certificate issued by an entity accredited under national/international standards is not provided, such measuring equipment is required to be calibrated.

[CO$_2$ emission factor]

For grid electricity: The most recent value available from the source stated in this table at the time of validation

For captive electricity: Calculation from manufacturer's specification (Option a) or

the manufacturer (η_{elec} [%]).

Measured data of generated and supplied electricity by the captive power generation system including co-generation system ($EG_{PJ,p}$ [MWh/p]).

Data measured or provided by the fuel supplier of fuel amount consumed to generate heat and electricity by the captive power generation system including co-generation system ($FC_{PJ,p}$ [mass or weight/p]).

Net calorific value (NCV_{fuel} [GJ/mass or weight]) and CO$_2$ emission factor (EF_{fuel} [tCO$_2$/GJ]) of the fuel in order of preference:
1) values provided by the fuel supplier;
2) measurement by the project participants;
3) regional or national default values;
4) IPCC default values provided in table 1.4 of Ch.1 Vol.2 of 2006 IPCC Guidelines on National GHG Inventories. Lower value is applied.

with measured data (Option b) as follows:

Option a) Manufacturer's specification

The power generation efficiency (η_{elec}) based on lower heating value (LHV) of the captive power generation system including co-generation system from the manufacturer's specification is applied;

$$EF_{elec,ca,i} = 3.6 \times \frac{100}{\eta_{elec}} \times EF_{fuel,i}$$

Option b) Measured data

The monitored data of the amount of fuel input for power generation ($FC_{PJ,p}$) and the amount of electricity generated ($EG_{PJ,p}$) during the monitoring period p is applied. The measurement is conducted with the monitoring equipment to which calibration certificate is issued by an entity accredited under national/international standards;

$$EF_{elec,ca,i} = FC_{PJ,p} \times NCV_{fuel,i} \times EF_{fuel,i}$$
$$\times \frac{1}{EG_{PJ,p}}$$

Where:

$NCV_{fuel,i}$: Net calorific value of consumed fuel i [GJ/mass or weight]

$EF_{fuel,i}$: CO_2 emission factor of consumed fuel i [tCO$_2$/GJ]

History of the document

Version	Date	Contents revised
01.0	10 February 2017	JC6, Annex 5 Initial approval.

Joint Crediting Mechanism
Project Design Document Form

JCM_ID_F_PDD_ver01.1

JCM Project Design Document Form

A. Project description

A.1. Title of the JCM project

Reduction of Energy Consumption by Introducing an Energy-Efficient Waste Paper Processing System into a Packaging Paper Factory in Bekasi, West Java

A.2. General description of project and applied technologies and/or measures

The demand of paper has grown rapidly in Indonesia driven by its high economic growth. As one of the leading companies of corrugated carton production in Indonesia, PT FAJAR SURYA WISESA (Fajar Paper) decided to equip higher energy efficient technologies of Aikawa Iron Works than those for existing Line 5 in its newly built production Line 8 as a JCM project.

A corrugated carton production process consists of the following two main processes: old corrugated cartons (OCC) process and sheet forming process. This project aims to reduce electric power use in the former process.

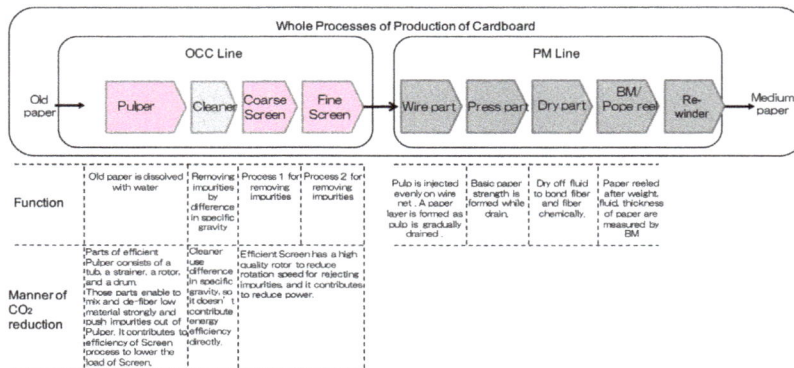

Figure 1: OCC process in the entire cardboard production processes

In the OCC process, the material of sheet paper is made by removing foreign substances, using multiple machines from ground and then liquefied old paper with water. This process is composed of 4 components based 30 equipment. It is expected the specific energy consumption of the project OCC Line 8 is around 0.12 MWh/ton (for 1,400 ton/day), in comparison to the historical performance of the existing OCC Line 5 (0.188 MWh/ton) whose output product is the same of the Line 8.

1

JCM_ID_F_PDD_ver01.1

A.3. Location of project, including coordinates

Country	Indonesia
Region/State/Province etc.:	Jawa Barat/ Bekasi
City/Town/Community etc:	Cikarang Bar/ Kalijaya/ Jl. Kampung Gardu Sawah No. 1
Latitude, longitude	16°16'20"S 107°07'22"E

A.4. Name of project participants

The Republic of Indonesia	PT FAJAR SURYA WISESA Tbk.
Japan	KANEMATSU CORPORATION

A.5. Duration

Starting date of project operation	1 April 2017
Expected operational lifetime of project	12 years

A.6. Contribution from Japan

The proposed project was partially supported by the Ministry of the Environment, Japan (MOEJ) through the Financing Programme for JCM Model projects, which provided financial support of less than half of the initial investment for the projects in order to acquire JCM credits. The Japanese project participant transfers the technology through conducting the training on operation and maintenance of newly installed equipment through this project.

B. Application of an approved methodology(ies)

B.1. Selection of methodology(ies)

Selected approved methodology No.	ID_AM012
Version number	1.0

B.2. Explanation of how the project meets eligibility criteria of the approved methodology

Eligibility criteria	Descriptions specified in the methodology	Project information
Criterion 1	The specific energy consumption of the project OCC line guaranteed by the manufacture is, at the	Project specific energy consumption (0.120 MWh/ton for 1,400 ton/day) for Line 8 expected by Aikawa Iron Works is less than historical performance of Line 5 (0.188 MWh/ton) which produces

2

JCM_ID_F_PDD_ver01.1

	minimum, less than the reference specific energy consumption set for the project factory.	equivalent product. [Note: ton implies BDt (Bone Dry ton)]
Criterion 2	The paper yield of the project OCC line(s) guaranteed by the manufacture is equal to or more than 90% at the range of designed production capacity.	The guaranteed paper yield is 92% in the project OCC line 8 as shown in "6.4.4.2. Fiber Loss Amount" of the "Technical guarantees" provided by Aikawa Iron Works,
Criterion 3	Production capacity of the project OCC line is no more than the twice as large as the capacity of the existing OCC line	Project capacity of the OCC Line (1,400 ton/day) is less than the twice as large as 1,150 ton/day, which is the maximum capacity of existing OCC line 5 which produces equivalent product.
Criterion 4	Plan for regular adjustment, replacement, and improvements of project OCC line(s) are prepared (at least once every six months).	Aikawa Iron Works agreed with Fajar to give the appropriate advices for the stable operation of the Line 8 every 3 months with the visit at least every 6 months (Agreement signed on August 28, 2015).

C. Calculation of emission reductions

C.1. All emission sources and their associated greenhouse gases relevant to the JCM project

Reference emissions	
Emission sources	GHG type
Electricity consumption by the reference OCC line(s)	CO_2
Project emissions	
Emission sources	GHG type
Electricity consumption by the project OCC line(s)	CO_2

C.2. Figure of all emission sources and monitoring points relevant to the JCM project

Monitoring Points in Whole Process

For monitoring, Fajar uses energy management system "DCS" and reporting system "SAP".

At this factory, Line 8 has its energy monitoring/control room. It collects and records monitored electricity consumption of each facility of the OCC line every hour.

Fajar monitors electricity consumption and paper production weight. For electricity, data of Pulper, Coarse Screen and Fine Screen are only measured. Paper production weight is measured by weight bridge at the last process. Both electricity and paper production (Gross) are

JCM_ID_F_PDD_ver01.1

automatically monitored.

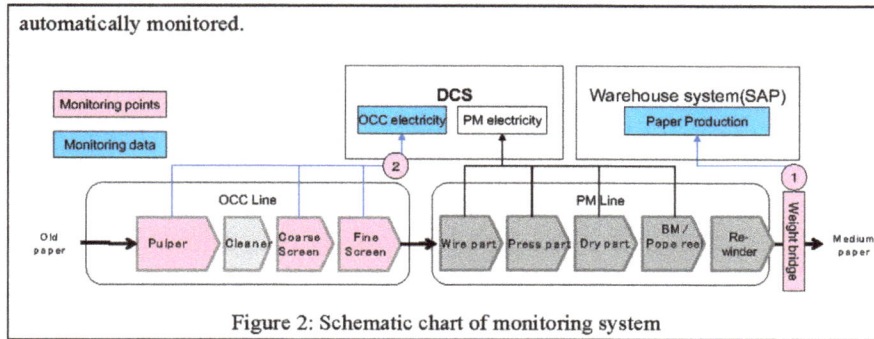

Figure 2: Schematic chart of monitoring system

C.3. Estimated emissions reductions in each year

Year	Estimated Reference emissions (tCO$_{2e}$)	Estimated Project Emissions (tCO$_{2e}$)	Estimated Emission Reductions (tCO$_{2e}$)
2017	39,433.5	25,174.8	14,258
2018	52,578.0	33,566.4	19,011
2019	52,578.0	33,566.4	19,011
2020	52,578.0	33,566.4	19,011
Total (tCO$_2$e)	197,167.5	125,874.0	71,291

[Note] The emission reductions are counted from April 1, 2017.

D. Environmental impact assessment

Legal requirement of environmental impact assessment for the proposed project	YES. In addition to the EIA (UKL-UPL) obtained in 2015 (660.2.1/084/TL&ADL/BPLH), Fajar owns the Environmental Permit (Nomor: 503.9.a/Kep 127/ BPMPPT/V/2015). EIA (UKL-UPL) is governed by the Indonesian Law Number 32 (2009). While the Environmental Permit is governed by Government Regulation Number 27 (2012). Both the Permit and EIA complement each other.

E. Local stakeholder consultation

E.1. Solicitation of comments from local stakeholders

Local Stakeholder Consultation (LSC) had been held in 20th December, 2016, which had invited several stakeholder; Staff of Fajar Paper, Indonesian Government and Indonesian Pulp and Paper

4

JCM_ID_F_PDD_ver01.1

Association.

Date/Location

Date: 20 December, 2016
Venue: Mill site of PT FAJAR SURYA WISESA Tbk.

LSC Agenda

10:00~10:15: Time adjustment
10:15~10:20: Opening remarks by Mr. Roy of Fajar
10:20~10:30: Introduction of relative entities
10:30~10:50: JCM introduction by Yoshimoto of NRI
10:50~11:00: JCM in Indonesia by Ms. Keni of JCM secretariat
11:00~11:20: Introduction of Fajar and Line 8 by Mr. Hardy of Fajar
11:20~11:40: JCM boundary and Equipment of JCM project by Mr. Aoshima of Aikawa Iron Works
11:40~11:45: Q&A
11:45~11:50: Closing by Mr. Asami of Kanematsu
12:00~13:00: Lunch organized by Fajar
13:00~14:00: Mill site tour organized by Fajar

List of Participants,

Organization
FajarPaper
Kanematsu
Aikawa Iron Works
Nomura Research Institute
SUNCOSMO
JCM secretariat
Coordinating Ministry of Economic Affairs
Ministry of Industry
APKI(Indonesian Pulp and Paper Association)

E.2. Summary of comments received and their consideration

Stakeholders	Comments received	Consideration of comments received
Director of Fajar	Japanese stakeholders involved into this project	No Action

5

JCM_ID_F_PDD_ver01.1

Paper	is appreciated and the enthusiasm for utilizing and further promoting JCM is mentioned.	
Indonesia JCM secretariat	This project is positioned as a first project of paper industry in Indonesia and an important project. Moreover, in order to develop the project horizontally to other paper factories in Indonesia, it is pointed to set up committees involving public and private sectors in the paper industry and to appeal the results of this JCM project.	No Action
the Ministry of Industry	An introduction about the efforts of the paper industry in the Ministry of Industry is given. The energy reduction amount by the project OCC was asked.	No Action
Indonesian pulp and paper Association	The total production capacity and yield of LINE 8 was asked.	No Action

F. References

– UKL-UPL report (660.2.1/084/TL&ADL/BPLH)
– Environmental permit (Nomor: 503.9.a/Kep 127/ BPMPPT/V/2015)

Reference lists to support descriptions in the PDD, if any.

Annex

–

Revision history of PDD

Version	Date	Contents revised
0.1	13/02/2017	Initial draft.
1.0	18/09/2017	Revised for validation.
1.1	22/09/2017	Revised for validation
1.2	27/11/2017	Revision with revised emission factors

6

Monitoring Plan

Monitoring Plan Sheet (Input Sheet) [Attachment to Project Design Document]

Table 1: Parameters to be monitored *ex post*

		1	2
(a)	Monitoring point No.	1	2
(b)	Parameters	$PP_{j,p}$	$EC_{PJj,p}$
(c)	Description of data	Paper production measured at the PM line connected to the project OCC line *j* during the period *p*	Electricity consumption by the project OCC line *j* during the period *p*
(e)	Units	ton/p	MWh/p
(f)	Monitoring option	Option C	Option C
(g)	Source of data	Monitored data	Monitored data
(h)	Measurement methods and procedures	Measuring equipment is installed to the PM line connected to the project OCC line j—*for this project, the project line is unique, so the suffix j is omitted*— to measure volume of paper production. Measurement is conducted as follows: - Measured data is automatically transmitted to the remote server/PC for recording. - Data recorded in the remote server/PC is reported and double-checked by a responsible staff on a monthly basis to prevent missing data. In case a calibration certificate issued by an entity accredited under national/international standards is not provided, such measuring equipment is required to be calibrated base on the national regulation or manufacturer's recommendations.	Measuring equipment is installed to the project OCC line j—for this project, the project line is unique, so the suffix j is omitted—to measure electricity consumption. Electricity consumption of the OCC line is measured with measuring equipments. - Measured data is automatically transmitted to the remote server/PC for recording. - Data recorded in the remote server/PC is reported and double-checked by a responsible staff on a monthly basis to prevent missing data. In case a calibration certificate issued by an entity accredited under national/international standards is not provided, such measuring equipment is required to be calibrated.
(i)	Monitoring frequency	Monitored hourly and recorded monthly for aggregation. The estimated value below is annual one.	Monitored hourly and recorded monthly for aggregation. The estimated value below is annual one.
(j)	Other comments	Compiled data is to be stored electronically after 2 years beyond the end of the JCM project. "ton" implies "BDt (Bone Dry ton)". Weight bridge is to be calibrated as specified in its certificate. It is to be calibrated in accordance with the International Recommendation (OIML R 76-1: 2006).	Compiled data is to be stored electronically after 2 years beyond the end of the JCM project. Electricity meter does not require additional calibration as specified in its specs.
(d)	**Estimated Value**		
	i=1	420,000	50,400
	i=2		
	i=3		
	i=4		
	i=5		
	i=6		
	i=7		
	i=8		
	i=9		
	i=10		

[Monitoring option]

Option A	Based on public data which is measured by entities other than the project participants (Data used: publicly recognized data such as statistical data and specifications)
Option B	Based on the amount of transaction which is measured directly using measuring equipments (Data used: commercial evidence such as invoices)
Option C	Based on the actual measurement using measuring equipments (Data used: measured values)

Table 2: Project-specific parameters to be fixed *ex ante*

(a)	Parameters	EF_{elec}	SEC_{RE}
(b)	Description of data	CO_2 emission factor for consumed electricity	Reference specific electricity consumption of the OCC line
(d)	Units	tCO_2/MWh	MWh/ton
(e)	Source of data	[Grid electricity] The most recent value available at the time of validation is applied and fixed for the monitoring period thereafter. The data is sourced from "Emission Factors of Electricity Interconnection Systems", National Committee on Clean Development Mechanism (Indonesian DNA for CDM), based on data obtained by Directorate General of Electricity, Ministry of Energy and Mineral Resources, Indonesia, unless otherwise instructed by the Joint Committee." [Captive electricity] Specification of the captive power generation system including co-generation system provided by the manufacturer. Net calorific value (NCVfuel [GJ/mass or weight]) and CO2 emission factor (EFfuel [tCO2/GJ]) of the fuel (EFfuel [tCO2/GJ]) from IPCC as follows. IPCC default values provided in table 1.4 of Ch.1 Vol.2 of 2006 IPCC Guidelines on National GHG Inventories. Lower value is applied.	Data of daily electricity consumption by the OCC line and daily weight of paper product at the PM line connected to the OCC line within two years from the timing of validation of the existing OCC lines at the same factory where the project OCC line(s) is installed.
(f)	Other comments	Grid and a gas-based captive power supplies electricity to the facility. Base on the historical (2014) data of ratio of both sources and technical specification of the latter are used to calculate the combined CO2 emission factor of the electricity which is fixed ex ante as per the methodology.	The Line 5 historical data (2016) are used for calculation. The relevant calculation is given by another file.
(c)	Estimated Value		
	i=1	0.666	0.188
	i=2		
	i=3		
	i=4		
	i=5		
	i=6		
	i=7		
	i=8		
	i=9		
	i=10		

Table 3: *Ex-ante* estimation of each CO_2 emission reduction

(a)	Parameters	$RE_{j,p}$	$PE_{j,p}$	$ER_{j,p}$
(b)	Description of data	Reference emissions of the OCC line j during the period p	Project emissions of the OCC line j during the period p	Emission reductions of the OCC line j during the period p
(d)	Units	tCO_2/p	tCO_2/p	tCO_2/p
(c)	Estimated Value			
	j=1	52,578.0	33,566.4	19,011.6
	j=2	0.0	0.0	0.0
	j=3	0.0	0.0	0.0
	j=4	0.0	0.0	0.0
	j=5	0.0	0.0	0.0
	j=6	0.0	0.0	0.0
	j=7	0.0	0.0	0.0
	j=8	0.0	0.0	0.0
	j=9	0.0	0.0	0.0
	j=10	0.0	0.0	0.0

Table 4: *Ex-ante* estimation of CO_2 emission reductions

CO_2 emission reductions	Units
19,011	tCO_2/p

APPENDIX 5
Joint Crediting Mechanism Validation Report Form

JCM Validation Report Form

A. Summary of validation	

A.1. General Information

Title of the project	Reduction of Energy Consumption by Introducing an Energy-Efficient Waste Paper Processing System into a Packaging Paper Factory in Bekasi, West Java
Reference number	ID 011
Third-party entity (TPE)	Japan Quality Assurance Organization (JQA)
Project participant contracting the TPE	KANEMATSU CORPORATION
Date of completion of this report	29/11/2017

A.2 Conclusion of validation

Overall validation opinion	☒ Positive
	☐ Negative

A.3. Overview of final validation conclusion

Only when all of the checkboxes are checked, overall validation opinion is positive.

Item	Validation requirements	No CAR or CL remaining
Project design document form	The TPE determines whether the PDD was completed using the latest version of the PDD forms appropriate to the type of project and drafted in line with the Guidelines for Developing the Joint Crediting Mechanism (JCM) Project Design Document, Monitoring Plan and Monitoring Report.	☒
Project description	The description of the proposed JCM project in the PDD is accurate, complete, and provides comprehension of the proposed JCM project.	☒
Application of approved JCM methodology (ies)	The project is eligible for applying applied methodology and that the applied version is valid at the time of submission of the proposed JCM project for validation.	☒
Emission sources and calculation of emission reductions	All relevant GHG emission sources covered in the methodology are addressed for the purpose of calculating project emissions and reference emissions for the proposed JCM project.	☒
	The values for project specific parameters to be fixed *ex ante* listed in the Monitoring Plan Sheet are appropriate, if applicable.	☒
Environmental impact assessment	The project participants conducted an environmental impact assessment, if required by the Republic of Indonesia, in line with Indonesia's procedures.	☒
Local stakeholder	The project participants have completed a local stakeholder consultation process and that due steps were taken to engage	☒

1

JCM_ID_F_Val_Rep_ver01.0

Item	Validation requirements	No CAR or CL remaining
consultation	stakeholders and solicit comments for the proposed project unless a local stakeholder consultation has been conducted under an environmental impact assessment.	
Monitoring	The description of the Monitoring Plan (Monitoring Plan Sheet and Monitoring Structure Sheet) is based on the approved methodology and/or Guidelines for Developing the Joint Crediting Mechanism (JCM) Project Design Document, Monitoring Plan, and Monitoring Report. The monitoring points for measurement are appropriate, as well as whether the types of equipment to be installed are appropriate if necessary.	☒
Public inputs	All inputs on the PDD of the proposed JCM project submitted in line with the Project Cycle Procedure are taken into due account by the project participants.	☒
Modalities of communications	The corporate identity of all project participants and a focal point, as well as the personal identities, including specimen signatures and employment status, of their authorized signatories are included in the MoC.	☒
	The MoC has been correctly completed and duly authorized.	☒
Avoidance of double registration	The proposed JCM project is not registered under other international climate mitigation mechanisms.	☒
Start of operation	The start of the operating date of the proposed JCM project does not predate January 1, 2013.	☒

Authorised signatory:		Mr. ☒	Ms. ☐
Last name: Asada		First name: Sumio	
Title: Senior Executive			
Specimen signature:			Date: 29/11/2017

2

JCM_ID_F_Val_Rep_ver01.0

B. Validation team and other experts

	Name	Company	Function*	Scheme competence*	Technical competence*	On-site visit
Mr. ☒ Ms. ☐	Tadashi Yoshida	JQA	Team leader	☒	Authorized	☒
Mr. ☒ Ms. ☐	Koichiro Tanabe	JQA	Technical Reviewer	☒	Authorized	☐
Mr. ☐ Ms. ☐				☐		☐
Mr. ☐ Ms. ☐				☐		☐

Please specify the following for each item.

* *Function: Indicate the role of the personnel in the validation activity such as team leader, team member, technical expert, or internal reviewer.*
* *Scheme competence: Check the boxes if the personnel have sufficient knowledge on the JCM.*
* *Technical competence: Indicate if the personnel have sufficient technical competence related to the project under validation.*

C. Means of validation, findings, and conclusion based on reporting requirements

C.1. Project design document form

\<Means of validation\>

The PDD form was checked and confirmed as complete in accordance with the JCM Guidelines for Developing Project Design Document and Monitoring Report (JCM_ID_GL_ PDD_MR_ver02.1). A valid form of the JCM PDD form (JCM_ID_F_PDD_ver01.1) is used for the PDD of the proposed project (Version 0.1 dated 13/02/2017 for Initial draft and Version 1.2 dated 27/11/2017 for the final PDD). The validation was conducted on the initial draft of the PDD.

\<Findings\>

Please state if CARs, CLs, or FARs are raised, and how they are resolved.

No issues were identified to the requirement.

\<Conclusion based on reporting requirements\>

Please state conclusion based on reporting requirements.

JQA concludes that the PDD is completed using the latest version of the PDD form and drafted in line with the JCM Guidelines for Developing the JCM Project Design Document, Monitoring Plan and Monitoring Report.

JCM_ID_F_Val_Rep_ver01.0

C.2. Project description

<Means of validation>

The purpose of the proposed project is to reduce CO_2 emissions from electricity consumption in the corrugated carton process of the packaging paper factory. The cardbord making process consists of mainly corrugated carton process (OCC process) and sheet forming process (PM process). In the proposed project, to achieve the reduction of electricity consumption in the OCC process per unit of paper production, PT Fajar Surya Wisesa Tbk, which is located in Cikarang Bar, Indonesia and is one of the leading companies of corrugated carton production in Indonesia, has decided to introduce higher energy-efficient technology from Aikawa Iron Works Co., Ltd. into an OCC line (Line 8) newly installed as a JCM project. The new technology provides less electricity consumption in the operation of the OCC line compared to the existing OCC line (Line 5) which is similar to Line 8 in the product.

In the OCC process consisting of four main components, the recycled waste paper is first liquefied with water by the use of pulper where the foreign substances such as plastics and others are removed, and then followed by the coarse/fine screen processes to remove small amounts of impurities from the material of paper sheet supplied to the next PM process. Thus, the installation of new pulper and coarse/fine screens with higher efficiency contributes to the great reduction of electricity consumption in the OCC line and the annual emission reductions of 19,011 tCO2/yr would be achieved by the proposed JCM project.

The project is implemented by PT Fajar Surya Wisesa Tbk. from the Republic of Indonesia and Kanematsu Corporation from Japan. The commissioning date of project facilities was 19/12/2016, which is supported by Start-Up Certificate signed by PT Fajar Surya Wisesa Tbk. and Kanematsu Corporation, and the starting date of the project monitoring activity was 01/04/2017, which is confirmed by the monitoring data collected from this date. The expected operational lifetime of the project is 12 years which is based on the legal durable years list issued by Ministry of Finance, Japan.

The project is partially supported by the Ministry of the Environment, Japan (MOEJ) through the Financing programme for JCM Model projects, which provided financial support of less than half of the initial investment for the projects in order to acquire JCM credits. As for technology transfer, Aikawa Iron Works Co., Ltd. has conducted OJT training on the operation and maintenance of newly installed equipments at the project site. The maintenance service after project operation start will be provided by Aikawa Iron Works Co., Ltd. It also contributes to technical transfer to the staff of PT Fajar Surya Wisesa Tbk. through maintenance experiences.

JQA has assessed the revised PDD and the supporting documents and conducted an on-site

4

inspection to validate the requirements about accuracy and completeness of the project description.   The details of the persons interviewed and documents reviewed are provided in Section E of this report.

<Findings>

Please state if CARs, CLs, or FARs are raised, and how they are resolved.

No issue was raised to the requirement.

<Conclusion based on reporting requirements>

Please state conclusion based on reporting requirements.

JQA concludes that the description of the proposed JCM project in the revised PDD complies with the supporting documents and information obtained through the on-site visit and the interview with the PPs, and the description contained in the PDD is accurate, complete, and provides comprehension of the proposed JCM project.

C.3. Application of approved methodology(ies)

<Means of validation>

The approved methodology JCM_ID_AM012_ver01.0 "Reduction of Energy Consumption by Introducing an Energy-Efficient Old Corrugated Carton Processing System into a Cardboard Factory, Version 1.0" is applied to the proposed project.   The methodology is approved by the JC on 20/02/2017 (JC6, Annex 5) and valid at the time of the validation.

JQA assessed whether the selected methodology was applicable to the proposed project. The project applicability was checked against four eligibility criteria contained in the approved methodology.   The steps taken to validate each eligibility criterion and the conclusion about its applicability to the proposed project are summarized as follows:

Criterion 1: The specific energy consumption of the project OCC line guaranteed by the manufacture is, at the minimum, less than the reference specific energy consumption set for the project factory.

Justification in the PDD : Project specific energy consumption of Line 8 (0.120 MWh/ton for 1,400 ton/day) expected by Aikawa Iron Works is less than historical performance of Line 5 (0.188 MWh/ton) which produces equivalent product.   [Note: ton implies BDt (Bone dry ton)]

Assessment and conclusion : It is confirmed through the review of the relevant documents provided by Aikawa Iron Works and the on-site inspection that the sum of the rated electricity consumption of equipments newly installed for the OCC Line 8 is 6,992.8 kW (6.993 MW) and the yield of daily paper production of Line 8 is 1,400 ton/day.   Hence, the project specific

5

energy consumption of Line 8 gives 0.120 kWh/ton- paper production (= 6.993 MW x 24 hr/1,400 ton). This value is less than 0.188 MWh/ton of the reference OCC Line 5 which produces the similar paper product with Line 8.

Regarding the energy saving effect of Line 8 and the determination of reference specific electricity consumption, JQA raised CL 01 and CL 02 and these issues were resolved as explained in "Findings".

Criterion 2 : The paper yield of the project OCC line(s) guaranteed by the manufacture is equal to or more than 90% at the range of designed production capacity.

Justification in the PDD : The guaranteed paper yield is 92% in the project OCC Line 8 as shown in "6.4.4.2. Fiber Loss Amount" of the "Technical guarantees" provided by Aikawa Iron Works.

Assessment and conclusion : It is confirmed through the review of the technical specification provided by Aikawa Iron Works, on-site inspection and the interview with the PPs that Line 8 guarantees the paper yield of more than 92% from the waste paper feedstock except the foreign substanstances such as plastics. Therefore, JQA concludes that the Criterion 2 is satisfied.

Criterion 3 : Production capacity of the project OCC line is no more than the twice as large as the capacity of the existing OCC line.

Justification in the PDD : Project capacity of the OCC line (1,400 ton/day) is less than the twice as large as 1,150 ton/day, which is the maximum capacity of existing OCC Line 5 which produces equivalent product.

Assessment and conclusion : It is confirmed through the review of technical specification provided by Aikawa Iron Works, on-site inspection and the interview with the PPs that the paper production capacity of Line 8 is 1,400 ton/day and the maximum capacity of the existing OCC Line 5 is 1,150 ton/day. Thus, the capacity of Line 8 is less than the twice as large as the capacity of Line 5. Therefore, JQA concludes that the Criterion 3 is satisfied.

Criterion 4 : Plan for regular adjustment, replacement, and improvement of project OCC line(s) are prepared (at least once every six months).

Justification in the PDD : Aikawa Iron Works agreed with Fajar to give the appropriate advices for the stable operation of the Line 8 every 3 months with the visit at least every 6 months (Agreement signed on August 28, 2015).

Assessment and conclusion : Under the contract (Contract No. 3200003832 dated 28/08/2015) between PT Fajar Surya Wisesa Tbk and Kanematsu Corporation for Line 8, Aikawa Iron Works Co., Ltd. and PT Fajar Surya Wisesa Tbk made agreement on 28/08/2015 that Aikawa Iron Works Co., Ltd. visits PT Fajar Surya Wisesa Tbk with a target frequency of once per 3 months to give the appropriate advices for the stable operational performance and parts replacement based on the equipment's inspections of Line 8. The frequency of the visit could be as many as at least once per six months and this Agreement is effective for the period of 12 years from the date indicated on the Start-up Certificate of Line 8 (i.e., 19/12/2016). It is confirmed through the review of these documents and the interview with the PPs that the plan for regular adjustment, replacement and improvement of Line 8 is prepared.

Regarding the service plan for the project OCC line, JQA raised CL 03 and this issue was resolved as explained in "Findings".

<Findings>
Please state if CARs, CLs, or FARs are raised, and how they are resolved.
CL 01

As for Criterion 1, project specific energy consumption of Line 8 gives energy saving of 36% (= (0.188-0.120)/ 0.188 x 100), which is much larger than the target value of 10%. This inconsistency is to be clarified.

Resolution of CL 01 by the PPs :

The description in A.2 of the PDD is clarified to avoid confusion due to the different definition of "reductions". It is confirmed through the review of the relevant documents and the interview with the PPs that the project specific electricity consumption of Line 8 (0.120 MWh/ton) for a capacity of 1,400 ton/day is guaranteed by Aikawa Iron Works Co., Ltd. and this value is apparently less than the historical performance of Line 5 (0.188 MWh/ton) which produces the equivalent product with Line 8. The operation of the highly efficient OCC line would contribute to the large reductions in the emission reductions. Thus, CL 01 is closed.

CL 02

As for Criterion 1, the reference specific electricity consumption based on data of Line 5 (SEC_RE) is calculated using the data of electricity consumption and paper production in 2013-2014. The PPs are requested to justify the use of 2013-2014 data of Line 5 in accordance with the requiement in the methodology ID_AM012_ver01.0.

Resolution of CL 02 by the PPs :

The calculation of SEC_RE is revised based on the data of 2016. The result is almost the same as that of 2013-2014. It is confirmed through the review of the 2016 data from Line 5, in accordance with the requirement of the methodology ID_AM012_ver01.0, that the re-calculated reference specific electricity consumption of the OCC Line 5 is 0.188 MWh/ton. Thus, CL 02 is closed.

CL 03

As for Criterion 4, the PPs are requested to provide the plan for regular adjustment, replacement, and improvements of the project OCC line(s).

Resolution of CL 03 by the PPs:

Aikawa Iron Works Co., Ltd. agreed with PT Fajar Surya Wisesa Tbk to give the appropriate advices for the stable operation of Line 8 every three months with the visit at least every six months (Agreement signed on 28/08/2015). It is confirmed through the review of the Agreement (Contract No. 3200003882 B) and the interview with the PPs that the plan for regular adjustment, replacement and improvements of the project OCC Line 8 was prepared through the agreement between Aikawa Iron Works Co., Ltd. and PT Fajar Surya Wisesa Tbk on 28/08/2015. Thus, CL 03 is closed.

<Conclusion based on reporting requirements>
Please state conclusion based on reporting requirements.

JQA concludes that the proposed project is eligible for applying the valid version of the approved methodology ID_AM012_ver01.0 and all eligibility criteria have been met by the proposed JCM project.

C.4. Emission sources and calculation of emission reductions

<Means of validation>

The proposed project aims to reduce the electricity consumption from the OCC line in the corrugated carton production process by introducing higher energy efficient technologies. The sources of GHG emissions are electricity consumption by the reference OCC line and the project OCC line. The annual electricity consumption by the project OCC line (Line 8) is estimated to be 50,400 MWh for the paper production of 420,000 ton/yr. There is captive power generators using natural gas on-site to supply electricity continuously to a packaging paper factory of PT Fajar Surya Wisesa Tbk. The gross heat rate of the generator is 11,660 kJ/kWh which is sourced from the manufacturer's specification. The proposed project consumes electricity from both the captive power plant and the grid (JAMALI grid system), and the ratio of electricity consumption from the captive power plant and the grid is 87.5% and 12.5%, respectively, based on the data in 2014.

The CO_2 emission factor of the grid electricity is determined as 0.903 tCO_2/MWh (ex-post) based on the latest data (2015), sourced from "Emission Factors of Electricity Interconnection Systems" published by National Committee on CDM Indonesian Designated

National Authority (DNA), based on data obtained by Directorate General of Electricity, Ministry of Energy and Mineral Resources, Indonesia. The CO_2 emission factor of the captive power plant using natural gas is determined as 0.633 tCO_2/MWh (= 11,660 kJ/kWh x 54.3 tCO_2/TJ x 10^{-6}), based on the manufacturer's specification and the 2006 IPCC lower value for emission factor of natural gas. Therefore, the combined CO_2 emission factor of electricity consumed by the proposed project is determined to be 0.666 tCO_2/MWh (= (0.903 x 0.125) + (0.633 x 0.875)).

The reference specific electricity consumption of the OCC line (SEC_RE) which is calculated ex-ante by using the historical data (more than 300 data sets) of the existing OCC Line 5 in 2016 is correctly determined to be 0.188 MWh/ton in accordance with the requirements of the approved methodology.

The GHG emission reductions during the period p are calculated by the following equations, in line with the approved methodology:

ER_p = RE_p - PE_p

$= \Sigma$ (EC_RE,j,p x EF_elec } - Σ (EC_PJ,j,p x EF_elec)

$= \Sigma$ (SEC_RE x PP_j,p x EF_elec) - Σ (EC_PJ,j,p x EF_elec)

The annual GHG emission reductions are calculated from the reference specific electricity consumption (SEC_RE) of the existing OCC Line 5, weight of paper production (PP_j,p), electricity consumption of the new OCC Line 8 (EC_PJ,j,p) and combined CO_2 emission factor of electricity consumed (EF_elec). The annual emission reductions are calculated as follows:

ER_p = (0.188 MWh/ton x 420,000 ton/yr x 0.666 tCO_2/MWh) - (50,400 MWh/yr x 0.666 tCO_2/MWh)

= 52,578.0 - 33,566.4

= 19011.6 tCO_2/yr

The proposed project was commissioned on 19/12/2016 and started monitoring activity on 01/04/2017 after test operation. The GHG emission reductions in 2017 are estimated to be 14,258 tCO_2 and the sum of the emission reductions up to 2020 is estimated to be 71,291 tCO_2.

It is confirmed through the review of relevant documents and on-site inspection that all GHG emission sources specified by the applied methodology are identified, and the reference emissions, project emissions and emission reductions in the PDD_(ver.1.2) and Monitoring Plan Sheet are correctly calculated, in accordance with the methodology ID_AM012.ver01.0.

Regarding the parameters to be provided in MPS, JQA raised CAR 04 and this issue was resolved as explained in "Findings".

<Findings>

Please state if CARs, CLs, or FARs are raised, and how they are resolved.

CAR 04

JCM_ID_F_Val_Rep_ver01.0

The parameters necessary to calculate the reference and project emissions such as SEC_RE, PP_j,p, EF_elec, EC_PJ.j.p, are not provided in the cell of MPS (calc_process) sheet.

Resolution of CAR 04 by the PPs :

The sheet of MPS (calc_process) is protected and does not allow the users to edit them, just referring the results from the previous sheet.   It is confirmed through the review of the MPS approved by the Joint Committee that the sheet is protected not to edit by the users.   Thus, CAR 04 is closed.

<Conclusion based on reporting requirements>
Please state conclusion based on reporting requirements.

JQA concludes that all relevant GHG emission sources covered in the approved methodology are addressed for the purpose of calculating project emissions, reference emissions and emission reductions for the proposed JCM project and the values for the project specific parameters to be fixed ex-ante listed in the Monitoring Plan Sheet are correctly determined.

C.5. Environmental impact assessment

<Means of validation>

The proposed project introduces an energy-efficient waste paper processing system into a packaging paper factory to reduce electricity consumption by the OCC line in a corrugated carton production process.   The PDD states that an environmental impact assessment is required by laws of the host country.   According to Environmental Protection and Management Act (EPMA) No.32/2009, there are three categories of environmental management and reporting, depending on the significance of the environmental impacts of project activity, i.e. AMDAL (Environmental Impact Assessment), UKL/UPL (Environmental Management and Monitoring) and SPPL (Statement and Management Capability).

The proposed project is classified into UKL/UPL because of no significant impacts on the environment.   The UKL/UPL report was submitted to Environmental Management Bureau of Bekasi local government by PT Fajar Surya Wisesa Tbk on 29/01/2015 and approved with approval letter (660.2.1./084/TL&ADL/BPLH) on 01/04/2015.   In addition , the PPs got Environmental Permit (503.9.a/Kep 127/BPMPPT/V/2015) from Investment Board and Integrated Licensing Services of Government of Bekasi Regency on 06/05/2015, under the Government regulation of No. 27/2012.

It is confirmed through the review of the relevant documents and the interview with the PPs that the proposed project has no significant impacts on the environment and therefore

10

UKL/UPL report was successfully approved by the local government.

Regarding the conclusion of environmental assessment, Jqa raised CAR 01 and this issue was resolved as explained in "Findings".

<Findings>
Please state if CARs, CLs, or FARs are raised, and how they are resolved.
CAR 01

The conclusion of environmental assessment shall be attached in case the PPs selected "Yes", in accordance with the Guideline of the PDD.

Resolution of CAR 01 by the PPs:

In addition to the EIA (UKL-UPL) obtained in 2015 (660.2.1/084/TL&ADL/BPLH), Fajar owns the Environmental Permit (Nomor: 503.9.a/Kep 127/ BPMPPT/V/2015). EIA (UKL-UPL) is governed by the Indonesian Law Number 32 (2009). While the Environmental Permit is governed by Government Regulation Number 27 (2012). Both the Permit and EIA complement each other. It is confirmed through the review of the relevant documents and the interview with the PPs that the proposed project has no significant impacts on the environment and therefore the UKL/UPL report was approved by the local government on 01/04/2015. In addition to this, Environmental Permit was issued by the local authority on 06/05/2015. Thus, CAR 01 is closed.

<Conclusion based on reporting requirements>
Please state conclusion based on reporting requirements.

JQA concludes that the PPs have conducted an environmental impact assessment (UKL/UPL) and got the approval and permit from the local authorities, in line with procedures as required by the Republic of Indonesia.

C.6. Local stakeholder consultation

<Means of validation>
The PPs conducted a local stakeholder consultation under an environmental impact assessment at the mill site of PT Fajar Surya Wisesa Tbk on 20/12/2016. Prior to the meeting, the opening notice of the local stakeholder consultation was distributed to the stakeholders. The name of the organization participated in the consultation are as follows:
- JCM Secretariat of Indonesia
- Coordinating Ministry of Economic Affairs
- Ministry of Industry

11

JCM_ID_F_Val_Rep_ver01.0

- Indonesian Pulp and Paper Association
- PT Fajar Surya Wisesa Tbk
- Kanematsu Corporation
- AAikawa Iron Works Co., Ltd.
- Nomura Research Institute
- SUNCOSMO

As there is no residence near the area where any environmental impact could be caused by the proposed project, the representative of the residents is not included in the participants. The local stakeholders provided positive comments for the proposed project. No negative issues that require actions to be taken by the PPs were raised through the consultation. It is confirmed through the review of the relevant documents and the interview with the PPs that the stakeholder consultation process was appropriately conducted to collect stakeholders' opinions about the project. The summary of the comments received in the consultation and due account of all comments taken by the PPs are fully described in the PDD.

\<Findings\>
Please state if CARs, CLs, or FARs are raised, and how they are resolved.
No issue was identified to the requirement.

\<Conclusion based on reporting requirements\>
Please state conclusion based on reporting requirements.
JQA concludes that the PPs have completed a local stakeholder consultation process under an environmental impact assessment and invited comments on the proposed project from the local stakeholders. The summary of the comments received is provided in the PDD in a complete manner and the PPs have taken due account of all the comments received and described this process in the PDD.

C.7. Monitoring

\<Means of validation\>
The description of the monitoring plan (Monitoring Plan Sheet and Monitoring Structure Sheet) is based on the approved methodology ID_AM012_ver01.0. Two monitoring parameters, i.e., paper production weight measured at the PM line connected to the project OCC line j during the period p (PP_j,p) and electricity consumption by the project OCC line j during the period p (EC_PJ,j,p), are measured by the weight bridge and electricity meter, respectively, and the measured data is automatically transmitted to the remote server/PC for recording. The monitoring point is located at the end of the PM line for paper production

weight and at the end of the OCC line for electricity consumption of pulper, coarse/fine screen processes, respectively.

The paper production weight and electricity consumption are monitored hourly and recorded monthly for aggregation and the data recorded is double-checked by a responsible staff on a monthly basis to prevent the missing of data.   The weight bridge is calibrated by a qualified entity (Government of Karawang, Industrial and Trade Service, Regional Technical Implementation Unit for Metrology Legal) every year in compliance with international recommendation OIML R 76-1:2002.   In case a calibration certificate issued by an entity accredited under national/ international standards is not provided at the time of verification, the weight bridge is required to be calibrated.   The periodic calibration of electricity meter, except a test for shipping, is not required according to the manufacturer's specification.

The data monitored and required for verification and issuance is kept and archived electronically for two years after the final issuance of credits.

The roles and responsibilities of the personnels are described in Monitoring Structure Sheet in accordance with the requirements of the applied methodology.   The monitoring structure consists of Project Director, Project Leader, Project Manager and Monitoring Manager. Monitoring Manager is responsible for monitoring, collecting and archiving of data as well as the calibration of the measuring equipment.   He reports the data to the Project Leader. Project Leader is reported the monitored data from Monitoring Manager and is responsible for the checking of the data.   Project Manager is a point of contact related to all JCM inquiries, including JCM Secretariat Indonesia.   He prepares the monitoring report.

It is confirmed through the review of the relevant documents and the interview with the PPs that the monitoring plan complies with the requirements of the approved methodology and the PPs will be able to implement the monitoring activity appropriately according to the monitoring plan.

Regarding the calibration information of measuring equipment and the archiving procedure of data, JQA raised CAR 02 and CAR 03 and these issues were resolved as explained in "Findings".

<Findings>
Please state if CARs, CLs, or FARs are raised, and how they are resolved.
 CAR 02
Following issues are raised:
1) The PPs are requested to provide information on calibration frequency of electricity meter and weight bridge in MPS, in accordance with the Guideline of the PDD (para. 31),
2) The PPs are requested to provide calibration certificate in case the electricity meter and weight bridge are already calibrated.

13

Resolution of CAR 02 by the PPs :

1) Weight bridge is to be calibrated annually in accordance with the international recommendation OIML R 76-1:2006.   The electricity meter does not require additional calibration as specified in the manufacturer's specification.

2) The calibration certificate of weight bridge in 2016 is provided.

It is confirmed through the review of the relevant documents and the interview with the PPs that the calibration of measuring equipment is conducted at the frequency specified in the manufacturer's specification or international recommendation.   Thus, CAR 02 is closed.

CAR 03

The PPs are requested to describe archiving procedures of data in MPS in accordance with the Guideline of the PDD (para. 28).

Resolution of CAR 03 by the PPs: It is mentioned in the MPS that "Compiled data is to be stored electronically for 2 years after the end of the JCM project."   It is confirmed through the review of the MPS that the description on the archiving procedures is added in MPS, in accordance with the PDD Guideline (para. 28). Thus, CAR 03 is closed.

<Conclusion based on reporting requirements>

Please state conclusion based on reporting requirements.

JQA concludes that the description of Monitoring Plan is based on the approved methodology and Guidelines for Developing the JCM project design document (PDD) and Monitoring Plan, and the monitoring points as well as monitoring equipment for measurement are also appropriate.   Thus, the PPs have demonstrated feasibility of the monitoring structure and their abilities to implement the monitoring activity appropriately.

C.8. Modalities of Communication

<Means of validation>

JQA obtained the MoC from the PPs on 16/08/2017 for review in which Kanematsu Corporation is nominated as the focal point entity.   The form used is the latest version (JCM_ID_F_MoC_ver01.0) at the time of validation.   The MoC is signed by the authorized representatives of all the PPs with the contact details on 23/06/2017.

JQA has checked the personal identities including specimen signatures and employment status of the authorized signatories directly through the interview with the PPs during the site-visit.   Primary authorized signaory of Kanematsu Corporation is Mr. Makoto Yokoshi,

JCM_ID_F_Val_Rep_ver01.0

Manager of Industrial Machinery & Plant Section, Plant & Ships Department and Alternate authorized signatory is Mr. Norio Asami, Assistant manager of the same department.   Primary authorized signatory of PT Fajar Surya Wisesa Tbk is Mr. Roy Teguh, Director and Alternate authorized signatory is Mr. Marco Hardy, Finance manager.   It is confirmed that all corporate and personal details including specimen signatures and the information contained in the MoC are valid and accurate as requested in the JCM Guidelines for Validation and Verification.

<Findings>
Please state if CARs, CLs, or FARs are raised, and how they are resolved.
No issue was raised to the requirement.

<Conclusion based on reporting requirements>
Please state conclusion based on reporting requirements.
JQA concludes that the MoC is completed using the latest version of the form and the information and the specimen signature of the PPs contained in the MoC are correct and sufficient, in compliance with the requirements of the JCM Guidelines.   It is demonstrated that the MoC has been correctly completed and dully authorized.

C.9. Avoidance of double registration

<Means of validation>
The representative of focal point entity, Mr. Makoto Yokoshi, Manager of Industrial Machinery & Plant Section, Plant & Ships Department of Kanematsu Corporation, declares in the MoC that the proposed project is not registered under any other international climate mitigation mechanism other than the JCM.   It is confirmed through the check of publicly available information of Clean Development Mechanism (CDM), Verified Carbon Standard (VCS), etc. that the proposed project is not registered under any other international climate mitigation mechanisms in terms of the name of entity, applied technology, scale and the location.

<Findings>
Please state if CARs, CLs, or FARs are raised, and how they are resolved.
No issue was raised to the requirement.

<Conclusion based on reporting requirements>
Please state conclusion based on reporting requirements.
JQA concludes that the proposed project is not registered under any other international

15

JCM_ID_F_Val_Rep_ver01.0

climate mitigation mechanisms and hence will not result in double counting of GHG emission reductions.

C.10. Start of operation

<Means of validation>

For the proposed project, the machine commissioning was completed on 19/12/2016 as agreed between Kanematsu Corporation and PT Fajar Surya Wisesa Tbk in Start-Up Certificate. After completing the Accceptance Test, the proposed project started monitoring activity on 01/04/2017. Furthermore, the staff training for operation, monitoring and maintenance of the system was conducted in June and August 2017. It is confirmed through the review of relevant documents, on-site inspection and the interview with the PPs that the starting date of the proposed project given in the PDD, 01/04/2017, is correct and the staff training for PT Fajar Surya Wisesa Tbk was appropriately implemented.

<Findings>

Please state if CARs, CLs, or FARs are raised, and how they are resolved.

No issue was raised to the requirement.

<Conclusion based on reporting requirements>

Please state conclusion based on reporting requirements.

JQA concludes that the starting date of project operation is 01/04/2017 and does not predate 01/01/2013 as required by the Guideline of the JCM project.

C.11. Other issues

<Means of validation>

There is no issue.

<Findings>

Please state if CARs, CLs, or FARs are raised, and how they are resolved.

Not applicable.

<Conclusion based on reporting requirements>

Please state conclusion based on reporting requirements.

Not applicable.

JCM_ID_F_Val_Rep_ver01.0

<table>
<tr><td></td></tr>
</table>

D. Information on public inputs

D.1. Summary of public inputs

In line with the JCM Project Cycle Procedure, the PDD was made publicly available for 30 days from 22/07/2017 to 20/08/2017 to invite public comments on the JCM website. https://www.jcm.go.jp/id-jp/information/70

No public comments were received.

D.2. Summary of how inputs received have been taken into account by the project participants

Not applicable

E. List of interviewees and documents received

E.1. List of interviewees

Mr. Wimba Wibawa Wanadiardja	Director, PT Fajar Surya Wisesa Tbk
Mr. Marco Hardy	Finance Manager, PT Fajar Surya Wisesa Tbk
Mr. Shandy Koeswanto	Corporate Finance, PT Fajar Surya Wisesa Tbk
Mr. Sarwi	Health Safety & Environment Division, PT Fajar Surya Wisesa Tbk
Mr. Naoki Matsuo	Senior Research Fellow, Climate Experts Ltd.

E.2. List of documents received

- PDD, version 0.1 13/02/2017, version 1.0 18/09/2017, version 1.2 27/11/2017.
- MPS and MSS, version 0.1 13/02/2017, version 1.0 18/09/2017, version 1.2 27/11/2017
- Methodology ID_AM012_ver01.0 approved on 10/02/2017 (JC6, Annex 5)
- Modalities of Communication, 30/06/2017
- Historical data of electricity consumption and paper production weight of Line 5 in 2016
- Process flow diagram of packaging paper factory including corrugated carton production process

JCM_ID_F_Val_Rep_ver01.0

- Flow diagram overview of the OCC process
- Plant layout of Fajar Paper PM8
- Feasibility Study Report on the proposed project (JCM FS Final Report), 2014:
    "Introduction of Energy-Efficient Old Corrugated Cartons Process at a Paper Factory".
- Fajar Paper 2016 Annual Report, including company's profile.
    http://www.fajarpaper.com/products/our-products
- Kanematsu Corporate Profile 2017   http://www.kanematsu.co.jp/en/
- Profile of Aikawa Iron Works Co., Ltd.   http://www.kanematsu.co.jp/en/
- Commissioning of stock preparation system for PM8 (Line 8), Start-up Certificate dated 19/12/2016
- Monitoring data of electricity consumption and paper production of Line 8 in April 2017 for starting date of project operation
- Legal durable years list issued by Ministry of Finance, Japan, for operational lifetime of the project
- List of equipment installed in Line 8 and the sum of electricity consumption
- Aikawa newest OCC treating system for corrugate medium in 2014
- Technical guarantees of Line 8 prepared by Aikawa Iron Works Co., Ltd.
- Supply contract (No. 3200003882-1) between PT Fajar Surya Wisesa Tbk and Kanematsu Corporation
- Maintenance plan agreed by Aikawa Iron Works Co., Ltd and PT Fajar Surya Wisesa Tbk dated 28/08/2015 (No. 3200003882 B)
- UKL/UPL (Environmental Management and Monitoring) of the proposed project submitted to Environmental Management Bureau of Bekasi local government on 29/01/2015
- Approval letter of UKL/UPL (660.2.1./084/TL&ADL/BPLH) on 01/04/2015.
- Environmental Permit (503.9.a/Kep 127/BPMPPT/V/2015) of the proposed project from Investment Board and Integrated Licensing Services of Government of Bekasi Regency on 06/05/2015
- Minutes of local stakeholder consultation held on 19/12/2016
- Presentation material for the local stakeholder consultation
- Schematic diagram of monitoring structure for the proposed project
- User guide - Power Logic TM PM5300 Series Power and Energy Meter issued by Schneider Electric
- Mettler Toledo - Terminals PLC Interface Manual IND131/IND331
- Calibration certificate of weight bridge issued by Government of Karawang, Industrial and Trade Service, Regional Technical Implementation Unit for Metrology Legal in 2016
- International Recommendation OIML R 76-1: 2006, Part 1- Metrological and technical requirements-Tests

18

JCM_ID_F_Val_Rep_ver01.0

- Training text - ABB DCS 800xA Industrial I
- Attendee list of training conducted in June and August 2017

19

JCM_ID_F_Val_Rep_ver01.0

Annex Certificates or curricula vitae of TPE's validation team members, technical experts and internal technical reviewers

Please attach certificates or curricula vitae of TPE's validation team members, technical experts and internal technical reviewers.

Statement of competence   JQA

Name   Dr. Tadashi Yoshida
Qualified and authorized by Japan Quality Assurance Organization

Function

	Date of qualification
Validator	2014/12/22
Verifier	2014/12/22
Team leader	2014/12/22

Technical area within sectoral scopes

	Date of qualification
TA 1.1 Thermal energy generation	2014/12/22
TA 1.2 Renewables	2014/12/22
TA 3.1 Energy demand	2014/12/22
TA 4.1 Cement and lime production	2015/11/12
TA 4.6 Other manufacturing industries	2014/12/22
TA 5.1 Chemical industry	2014/12/22
TA 10.1 Fugitive emissions from oil and gas	2014/12/22
TA 13.1 Solid waste and wastewater	2014/12/22
TA 14.1 Afforestation and reforestation	-

Statement of competence   JQA

Name   Mr. Koichiro Tanabe
Qualified and authorized by Japan Quality Assurance Organization

Function

	Date of qualification
Validator	-
Verifier	2014/12/22
Team leader	2014/12/22

Technical area within sectoral scopes

	Date of qualification
TA 1.1 Thermal energy generation	2014/12/22
TA 1.2 Renewables	2014/12/22
TA 3.1 Energy demand	2014/12/22
TA 4.1 Cement and lime production	-
TA 4.6 Other manufacturing industries	2014/12/22
TA 5.1 Chemical industry	2014/12/22
TA 10.1 Fugitive emissions from oil and gas	2014/12/22
TA 13.1 Solid waste and wastewater	2014/12/22
TA 14.1 Afforestation and reforestation	-

20

Monitoring Report Sheet (Input Sheet) [For Verification]

Table 1: Parameters monitored *ex post*

(a)	Monitoring period	01/07/2017–31/12/2017	01/07/2017–31/12/2017
(b)	Monitoring point No.	1	2
(c)	Parameters	$PP_{j,p}$	$EC_{PJ,j,p}$
(d)	Description of data	Paper production measured at the PM line connected to the project OCC line j during the period p	Electricity consumption by the project OCC line j during the period p
(e)	Units	ton/p	MWh/p
(f)	Monitoring option	Option C	Option C
(g)	Source of data	Monitored data	Monitored data
(h)	Measurement methods and procedures	Measuring equipment is installed to the PM line connected to the project OCC line j—for this project, the project line is unique, so the suffix j is omitted—to measure volume of paper production. Measurement is conducted as follows: - Measured data is automatically transmitted to the remote server/PC for recording. - Data recorded in the remote server/PC is reported and double-checked by a responsible staff on a monthly basis to prevent missing data. In case a calibration certificate issued by an entity accredited under national/international standards is not provided, such measuring equipment is required to be calibrated base on the national regulation or manufacturer's recommendations.	Measuring equipment is installed to the project OCC line j—for this project, the project line is unique, so the suffix j is omitted—to measure electricity consumption. Electricity consumption of the OCC line is measured with measuring equipments. - Measured data is automatically transmitted to the remote server/PC for recording. - Data recorded in the remote server/PC is reported and double-checked by a responsible staff on a monthly basis to prevent missing data.
(i)	Monitoring frequency	Monitored hourly and recorded monthly for aggregation.	Monitored hourly and recorded monthly for aggregation.
(j)	Other comments	Compiled data is to be stored electronically after 2 years beyond the end of the JCM project. "ton" implies "BDt (Bone Dry ton)". Weight bridge is to be calibrated as specified in its certificate. It is to be calibrated in accordance with the International Recommendation (OIML R 76-1: 2006).	Compiled data is to be stored electronically after 2 years beyond the end of the JCM project. Electricity meter does not require additional calibration as specified in its specs.
(k)	Monitored Value		
	j=1	109,777.0	11,914.2
	j=2		
	j=3		
	j=4		
	j=5		
	j=6		
	j=7		
	j=8		
	j=9		
	j=10		

[Monitoring option]

Option A	Based on public data which is measured by entities other than the project participants (Data used: publicly recognized data such as statistical data and specifications)
Option B	Based on the amount of transaction which is measured directly using measuring equipments (Data used: commercial evidence such as invoices)
Option C	Based on the actual measurement using measuring equipments (Data used: measured values)

Table 2: Project-specific parameters fixed *ex ante*

(a)	Parameters	EF_{elec}	SEC_{RE}
(b)	Description of data	CO_2 emission factor for consumed electricity	Reference specific electricity consumption of the OCC line
(c)	Units	tCO_2/MWh	MWh/ton
(d)	Source of data	[Grid electricity] The most recent value available at the time of validation is applied and fixed for the monitoring period thereafter. The data is sourced from "Emission Factors of Electricity Interconnection Systems", National Committee on Clean Development Mechanism (Indonesian DNA for CDM), based on data obtained by Directorate General of Electricity, Ministry of Energy and Mineral Resources, Indonesia, unless otherwise instructed by the Joint Committee." [Captive electricity] Specification of the captive power generation system including co-generation system provided by the manufacturer. Net calorific value (NCVfuel [GJ/mass or weight]) and CO2 emission factor (EFfuel [tCO2/GJ]) of the fuel (EFfuel [tCO2/GJ]) from IPCC as follows. IPCC default values provided in table 1.4 of Ch.1 Vol.2 of 2006 IPCC Guidelines on National GHG Inventories. Lower value is applied.	Data of daily electricity consumption by the OCC line and daily weight of paper product at the PM line connected to the OCC line within two years from the timing of validation of the existing OCC lines at the same factory where the project OCC line(s) is installed.
(e)	Other comments	Grid and a gas-based captive power supplies electricity to the facility. Base on the historical (2014) data of ratio of both sources and technical specification of the latter are used to calculate the combined CO2 emission factor of the electricity which is fixed ex ante as per the methodology.	The Line 5 historical data (2016) are used for calculation. The relevant calculation is given by another file.
(f)	Estimated Value		
	=1	0.666	0.188
	=2		
	=3		
	=4		
	=5		
	=6		
	=7		
	=8		
	=9		
	=10		

Table 3: *Ex-post calculation* of each CO_2 emission reduction

(a)	Parameters	$RE_{j,p}$	$PE_{j,p}$	$ER_{j,p}$
(b)	Description of data	Reference emissions of the OCC line *j* during the period *p*	Project emissions of the OCC line *j* during the period *p*	Emission reductions of the OCC line *j* during the period *p*
(d)	Units	tCO_2/p	tCO_2/p	tCO_2/p
(c)	Estimated Value			
	F1	13,742.5	7,934.8	5,807.7
	F2	0.0	0.0	0.0
	F3	0.0	0.0	0.0
	F4	0.0	0.0	0.0
	F5	0.0	0.0	0.0
	F6	0.0	0.0	0.0
	F7	0.0	0.0	0.0
	F8	0.0	0.0	0.0
	F9	0.0	0.0	0.0
	F10	0.0	0.0	0.0

Monitoring Spreadsheet JCM_ID_AM01
Reference Numb

Table 4: *Ex-post* calculation of CO_2 emission reductions

Monitoring period	CO_2 emission reductions
01/07/2017–31/12/2017	5,807

Monitoring Spreadsheet: JCM_ID_AM012_ver01.0
Reference Number: ID011

Monitoring Report Sheet (Calculation Process Sheet) [For Verification]

	Fuel type	Value	Units	Parameter
1. Calculations for emission reductions				
Emission reductions during the period *p*		5,807.7	tCO_2/p	ER_p
Emission reductions during the period *p*		5,807.7	tCO_2/p	ER_p
2. Selected default values, etc.				
3. Calculations for reference emissions				
Reference emissions during the period *p*		13,742.5	tCO_2/p	RE_p
Reference emissions during the period *p*	N/A	13,742.5	tCO_2/p	RE_p
4. Calculations of the project emissions				
Project emissions during the period *p*		7,934.8	tCO_2/p	PE_p
Project emissions during the period *p*	N/A	7,934.8	tCO_2/p	PE_p

Monitoring Report Sheet (Input Sheet) [For Verification]

Table 1: Parameters monitored *ex post*

(a)	Monitoring period	01/01/2018–31/08/2018	01/01/2018–31/08/2018
(b)	Monitoring point No.	1	2
(c)	Parameters	$PP_{j,p}$	$EC_{PU,j,p}$
(d)	Description of data	Paper production measured at the PM line connected to the project OCC line j during the period p	Electricity consumption by the project OCC line j during the period p
(e)	Units	ton/p	MWh/p
(f)	Monitoring option	Option C	Option C
(g)	Source of data	Monitored data	Monitored data
(h)	Measurement methods and procedures	Measuring equipment is installed to the PM line connected to the project OCC line j—for this project, the project line is unique, so the suffix j is omitted—to measure volume of paper production. Measurement is conducted as follows: - Measured data is automatically transmitted to the remote server/PC for recording. - Data recorded in the remote server/PC is reported and double-checked by a responsible staff on a monthly basis to prevent missing data. In case a calibration certificate issued by an entity accredited under national/international standards is not provided, such measuring equipment is required to be calibrated base on the national regulation or manufacturer's recommendations.	Measuring equipment is installed to the project OCC line j—for this project, the project line is unique, so the suffix j is omitted—to measure electricity consumption. Electricity consumption of the OCC line is measured with measuring equipments. - Measured data is automatically transmitted to the remote server/PC for recording. - Data recorded in the remote server/PC is reported and double-checked by a responsible staff on a monthly basis to prevent missing data.
(i)	Monitoring frequency	Monitored hourly and recorded monthly for aggregation.	Monitored hourly and recorded monthly for aggregation.
(j)	Other comments	Compiled data is to be stored electronically after 2 years beyond the end of the JCM project. "ton" implies "BDt (Bone Dry ton)". Weight bridge is to be calibrated as specified in its certificate. It is to be calibrated in accordance with the International Recommendation (OIML R 76-1: 2006).	Compiled data is to be stored electronically after 2 years beyond the end of the JCM project. Electricity meter does not require additional calibration as specified in its specs.
(k)	Monitored Value		
	j=1	172,090.0	16,775.8
	j=2		
	j=3		
	j=4		
	j=5		
	j=6		
	j=7		
	j=8		
	j=9		
	j=10		

[Monitoring option]

Option A	Based on public data which is measured by entities other than the project participants (Data used: publicly recognized data such as statistical data and specifications)
Option B	Based on the amount of transaction which is measured directly using measuring equipments (Data used: commercial evidence such as invoices)
Option C	Based on the actual measurement using measuring equipments (Data used: measured values)

Table 2: Project-specific parameters fixed *ex ante*

(a)	Parameters	EF$_{elec}$	SEC$_{RE}$
(b)	Description of data	CO$_2$ emission factor for consumed electricity	Reference specific electricity consumption of the OCC line
(c)	Units	tCO$_2$/MWh	MWh/ton
(d)	Source of data	[Grid electricity] The most recent value available at the time of validation is applied and fixed for the monitoring period thereafter. The data is sourced from "Emission Factors of Electricity Interconnection Systems", National Committee on Clean Development Mechanism (Indonesian DNA for CDM), based on data obtained by Directorate General of Electricity, Ministry of Energy and Mineral Resources, Indonesia, unless otherwise instructed by the Joint Committee." [Captive electricity] Specification of the captive power generation system including co-generation system provided by the manufacturer. Net calorific value (NCVfuel [GJ/mass or weight]) and CO2 emission factor (EFfuel [tCO2/GJ]) of the fuel (EFfuel [tCO2/GJ]) from IPCC as follows. IPCC default values provided in table 1.4 of Ch.1 Vol.2 of 2006 IPCC Guidelines on National GHG Inventories. Lower value is applied.	Data of daily electricity consumption by the OCC line and daily weight of paper product at the PM line connected to the OCC line within two years from the timing of validation of the existing OCC lines at the same factory where the project OCC line(s) is installed.
(e)	Other comments	Grid and a gas-based captive power supplies electricity to the facility. Base on the historical (2014) data of ratio of both sources and technical specification of the latter are used to calculate the combined CO2 emission factor of the electricity which is fixed ex ante as per the methodology.	The Line 5 historical data (2016) are used for calculation. The relevant calculation is given by another file.
(f)	Estimated Value		
	F1	0.666	0.188
	F2		
	F3		
	F4		
	F5		
	F6		
	F7		
	F8		
	F9		
	F10		

Table 3: *Ex-post calculation* of each CO_2 emission reduction

(a)	Parameters	$RE_{j,p}$	$PE_{j,p}$	$ER_{j,p}$
(b)	Description of data	Reference emissions of the OCC line *j* during the period *p*	Project emissions of the OCC line *j* during the period *p*	Emission reductions of the OCC line *j* during the period *p*
(d)	Units	tCO_2/p	tCO_2/p	tCO_2/p
(c)	Estimated Value			
	j=1	21,543.2	11,172.7	10,370.5
	j=2	0.0	0.0	0.0
	j=3	0.0	0.0	0.0
	j=4	0.0	0.0	0.0
	j=5	0.0	0.0	0.0
	j=6	0.0	0.0	0.0
	j=7	0.0	0.0	0.0
	j=8	0.0	0.0	0.0
	j=9	0.0	0.0	0.0
	j=10	0.0	0.0	0.0

Monitoring Spreadsheet JCM_ID_AM012_ver01.0
Reference Number: ID011

Table 4: *Ex-post* calculation of CO_2 emission reductions

Monitoring period	CO_2 emission reductions	Units
01/01/2018–31/08/2018	10,370	tCO_2/p

Monitoring Spreadsheet: JCM_ID_AM012_ver01.0
Reference Number: ID011

Monitoring Report Sheet (Calculation Process Sheet) [For Verification]					
1. Calculations for emission reductions		Fuel type	Value	Units	Parameter
Emission reductions during the period *p*			10,370.5	tCO_2/p	ER_p
	Emission reductions during the period *p*		10,370.5	tCO_2/p	ER_p
2. Selected default values, etc.					
3. Calculations for reference emissions					
Reference emissions during the period *p*			21,543.2	tCO_2/p	RE_p
	Reference emissions during the period *p*	N/A	21,543.2	tCO_2/p	RE_p
4. Calculations of the project emissions					
Project emissions during the period *p*			11,172.7	tCO_2/p	PE_p
	Project emissions during the period *p*	N/A	11,172.7	tCO_2/p	PE_p

Joint Crediting Mechanism Sustainable Development Implementation Report Form

JCM_ID_F_SDIR_ver01.0

JCM Sustainable Development Implementation Report Form

A. Project description

A.1. Title of the JCM project

Reduction of Energy Consumption by Introducing an Energy-Efficient Waste Paper Processing System into a Packaging Paper Factory in Bekasi, West Java

A.2. General information of project

Reference Number	ID011
Registration date	22nd December 2017
Monitoring period	01/07/2017-31/08/2018

B. Contribution to Sustainable Development

B.1 Check list for contribution to SD

No.	Items		Not identified	Identified	If "Identified" is checked in the box, please describe the corrective actions
1	EIA	Project is included in the EIA reporting to the Government of Indonesia	☐	☒	Environmental Permission updated in 2018
2	Pollution Control	Occurence of pollution in ambient air quality	☒	☐	
3		Occurence of pollution in water quality	☒	☐	
4		Occurence of waste generation	☒	☐	
5		Occurence of noise and/or vibration	☒	☐	
6		Occurence of ground subsidence	☒	☐	
7		Occurence of ambient odor	☒	☐	
8	Safety and health	Occurrence of accident or occupational accident	☒	☐	
9	Natural Environment and biodiversity	Change of protected area condition	☒	☐	
10		Change of land use change and ecosystem condition	☒	☐	
11		Introduction of foreign species	☒	☐	
12		Environmental impact during construction	☒	☐	
13		Use of surface water, ground water and/or deep ground water	☒	☐	
14	Economy	Decrease in local workforce capacity	☒	☐	
15		Declination of local community welfare	☒	☐	
16	Social Environment and Community Participation	Occurrence of resettlement or conflict	☒	☐	
17		Failure to follow up comments and complaints successfully	☒	☐	
18		Violation of regulatory working condition	☒	☐	
19	Technology	Failure to build human and institutional capacity by technology transter	☒	☐	
20		Failure to provide technology specification and manual book at least in English and in Bahasa Indonesia as applicable	☒	☐	

Joint Crediting Mechanism Verification Report Form

JCM_ID_F_Vrf_Rep_ver01.1

JCM Verification Report Form

A. Summary of verification

A.1. General Information

Title of the project	Reduction of Energy Consumption by Introducing an Energy-Efficient Waste Paper Processing System into a Packaging Paper Factory in Bekasi, West Java.
Reference number	ID011
Monitoring period	01/07/2017- 31/08/2018
Date of completion of the monitoring report	21/12/2018
Third-party entity (TPE)	Japan Quality Assurance Organization (JQA) (TPE-ID-003)
Project participant contracting the TPE	Kanematsu Corporation
Date of completion of this report	24/01/2019

A.2 Conclusion of verification and level of assurance

Overall verification opinion	☒ Positive ☐ Negative
☒ Unqualified opinion	Based on the process and procedure conducted, JQA provides reasonable assurance that the emission reductions for Reduction of Energy Consumption by Introducing an Energy-Efficient Waste Paper Processing System into a Packaging Paper Factory in Bekasi, West Java. ✓ Are free of material errors and are a fair representation of the GHG data and information, and ✓ Are prepared in line with the related JCM rules, procedure, guidelines, forms and other relevant documents
(If overall verification opinion is negative, please check below and state its reasons.) ☐ Qualified Opinion ☐ Adverse opinion ☐ Disclaimer	<State the reasons>

JCM_ID_F_Vrf_Rep_ver01.1

A.3. Overview of the verification results

Item	Verification requirements	No CAR or CL remaining
The project implementation with the eligibility criteria of the applied methodology	The TPE determines the conformity of the actual project and its operation with the eligibility criteria of the applied methodology.	☒
The project implementation against the registered PDD or any approved revised PDD	The TPE assesses the status of the actual project and its operation with the registered/validated PDD or any approved revised PDD.	☒
Calibration frequency and correction of measured values with related requirements	If monitoring Option C is selected, the TPE determines whether the measuring equipments have been properly calibrated in line with the monitoring plan and whether measured values are properly corrected, where necessary, to calculate emission reductions in line with the PDD and Monitoring Guidelines.	☒
Data and calculation of GHG emission reductions	The TPE assesses the data and calculations of GHG emission reductions achieved by/resulting from the project by the application of the selected approved methodology.	☒
Avoidance of double registration	The TPE determines whether the project is not registered under other international climate mitigation mechanisms.	☒
Post registration changes	The TPE determines whether there are post registration changes from the registered PDD and/or methodology which prevent the use of the applied methodology.	☒

Authorised signatory:	Mr. ☒ Ms. ☐
Last name: Asada	First name: Sumio
Title: Senior Executive	
Specimen signature:	Date: 24/01/2019

2

JCM_ID_F_Vrf_Rep_ver01.1

B. Verification team and other experts

		Name	Company	Function*	Scheme competence*	Technical competence*	On-site visit
Mr. ☒ Ms. ☐		Tadashi Yoshida	JQA	Team leader	☒	Authorized	☒
Mr. ☒ Ms. ☐		Hiroshi Motokawa	JQA	Internal reviewer	☒	Authorized	☐

Please specify the following for each item.

* *Function: Indicate the role of the personnel in the validation activity such as team leader, team member, technical expert, or internal reviewer.*

* *Scheme competence: Check the boxes if the personnel have sufficient knowledge on the JCM.*

* *Technical competence: Indicate if the personnel have sufficient technical competence related to the project under validation.*

C. Means of verification, findings and conclusions based on reporting requirements

C.1. Compliance of the project implementation and operation with the eligibility criteria of the applied methodology

<Means of verification>

The project was registered as a JCM project on 22/12/2017, which applied JCM approved methodology ID_AM012_ver01.0 "Reduction of Energy Consumption by Introducing an Energy-Efficient Old Corrugated Carton Processing System into a Cardboard Factory" under the scheme of Joint Crediting Mechanism between Republic of Indonesia and Japan.

The purpose of the project is to reduce CO_2 emissions from electricity consumption in the corrugated carton process of the packaging paper factory. The cardboard making process consists of mainly corrugated carton process (OCC line) and sheet forming process (PM line). In order to achieve the reduction of electricity consumption in the OCC process per unit of paper production, PT. Fajar Surya Wisesa Tbk. has introduced higher energy-efficient technology from Aikawa Iron Works Co., Ltd. into an OCC line (Line 8) newly installed as a JCM project. The new technology provides less electricity consumption in the operation of the OCC line (Line 8) compared to the existing OCC line (Line 5) while the new OCC line has produced 281,867 ton of the paper during the monitoring period.

The JCM website indicates that the starting date of the project operation is 01/04/2017 and this monitoring period is from 01/07/2017 to 31/08/2018. It is confirmed through the review of relevant documents, on-site assessment and the interview with the PPs that the monitoring actually started on 01/07/2017.

JQA has assessed whether the project implementation and operation during the monitoring

JCM_ID_F_Vrf_Rep_ver01.1

period complies with the eligibility criteria of the applied methodology.   After desk review, an on-site assessment was conducted on 21/12/2018.   JQA conducted a physical inspection and interviewed with the PPs listed in Section F of this verification report.

The assessment results regarding the eligibility criteria are summarized as below:

Criterion 1

The specific energy consumption of the project OCC line guaranteed by the manufacture is, at the minimum, less than the reference specific energy consumption set for the project factory.

Through the review of the monitored data and the interview with the PPs during on-site assessment, the project information of Criterion 1 in the PDD is confirmed as follows:

- Project specific energy consumption of Line 8 during the monitoring period was 0.1085 MWh/ton in 2017 and 0.0975 MWh/ton in 2018, which are much less than the reference specific energy consumption (SECRE) of 0.188 MWh/ton.

Hence, it is concluded that the project meets Criterion 1 with a satisfactory result during the monitoring period.

Criterion 2

The paper yield of the project OCC line(s) guaranteed by the manufacture is equal to or more than 90% at the range of designed production capacity.

Through the review of the monitored data and the interview with the PPs during on-site assessment, the project information of Criterion 2 in the PDD is confirmed as follows:

- The paper yield during the monitoring period was in a range of 97.1 – 99.5 %, which shows more than 90% at the range of designed production capacity.

Hence, it is concluded that the project meets Criterion 2 with a satisfactory result during the monitoring period.

Criterion 3

Production capacity of the project OCC line is no more than the twice as large as the capacity of the existing OCC line.

Through the review of the monitored data and the interview with the PPs during on-site assessment, the project information of Criterion 3 in the PDD is confirmed as follows:

- The amount of paper production by the OCC Line 8 during the monitoring period was 596.6 t/d in 2017 and 708.2 t/d in 2018, which are much less than the twice as large as 1,150 t/d which is the maximum capacity of the existing OCC Line 5.

Hence, it is concluded that the project meets Criterion 3 with a satisfactory result during the monitoring period.

Criterion 4

Plan for regular adjustment, replacement, and improvement of project OCC line(s) are prepared (at least once every six months).

Through the review of the maintenance records and the interview with the PPs during on-site assessment, the project information of Criterion 4 in the PDD is confirmed as follows:

- The maintenance records on the stable operation of the OCC Line 8 during the monitoring period was provided by the PPs. It is confirmed that PT. Fajar Surya Wisesa Tbk. was advised by Aikawa Iron Works several times during the monitoring period for the adjustment, replacement and improvement of the project OCC line, in accordance with the Agreement signed on 28/08/2015.

Hence, it is concluded that the project meets Criterion 4 with a satisfactory result during the monitoring period.

Regarding Criterion 4, JQA raised CL 03 and this issue was resolved as explained in "Findings".

<Findings>

Please state if CARs, CLs, or FARs are raised, and how they are resolved.

< CL 03 >

Regarding the Criterion 4 , the PP is requested to provide the records on the advice and maintenance/replacement for the stable operation of the OCC Line 8 during the monitoring period,

< Resolution of CL 03 by the PPs >

Following information is provided by the PPs:

The Aikawa Iron Works' staff members have visited several times to check and to recommend possible improvement and replacement, if any, of the machine operation. No specific recommendations was made which requires improvement and replacement of the OCC Line 8. It is confirmed through the review of the maintenance records and the interview with the PPs

JCM_ID_F_Vrf_Rep_ver01.1

that the OCC Line 8 has been appropriately operated and maintained during the monitoring period under Aikawa's advice and support. Thus, CL 03 is closed.

<Conclusion based on reporting requirements>
Please state conclusion based on reporting requirements.

JQA concludes that the implementation and the operation of the proposed project are in compliance with four eligibility criteria of the applied methodology ID_AM012 during this monitoring period.

C.2. Assessment of the project implementation against the registered PDD or any approved revised PDD

<Means of verification>

JQA has assessed the status of the actual project and its operation with the registered PDD through the review of the relevant documents, on-site inspection and interviews with the PPs. The project is implemented by the project participants of PT. Fajar Surya Wisesa Tbk. from Republic of Indonesia and Kanematsu Corporation from Japan.

The assessment results are summarized as follows;

[Physical features of the project]

PT. Fajar Surya Wisesa Tbk., who is one of the leading companies of corrugated carton production in Indonesia, has introduced higher energy-efficient paper recycle technology from Aikawa Iron Works Co., Ltd. into an OCC line (Line 8) newly installed as a JCM project in order to reduce electricity consumption in the OCC process. The new technology provides less electricity consumption in the operation of the OCC line (Line 8) compared to the existing OCC line (Line 5). The commissioning of the project equipment was completed on 19/12/2017. The installation of these equipment complies with the description of the registered PDD.

JQA confirms through the on-site inspection for the first verification that the physical features of the project are in place and the PPs have implemented the project as per the registered PDD.

[Monitoring points]

Two monitoring parameters described below are measured by weight bridge and electricity meter, respectively, in accordance with the monitoring plan.

JCM_ID_F_Vrf_Rep_ver01.1

1. $PP_{j,p}$: Paper production measured at the PM line j during the period p [ton/p]
2. $EC_{PJ,j,p}$: Electricity consumption by the project OCC line j during the period p [MWh/p]

It is confirmed through the on-site inspection and interview with the PPs that the weight bridge has been installed at the end of the PM line to measure paper production weight and electricity meter has been installed to measure electricity consumption from pulper and coarse/fine screens in the OCC line 8. These two measuring equipment are located at the right position, respectively.

The paper production weight and electricity consumption are monitored hourly and recorded monthly for aggregation. Measured data is automatically transmitted to the server and double-checked by a responsible staff on a monthly basis to prevent the missing of data. Detailed information on the monitoring data of these parameters is described in Section C.4.

[Monitoring structure]
The monitoring structure has been established and the roles and responsibilities of the personnel are consistent with the description in Monitoring Structure Sheet. The staff training for operation, monitoring and maintenance of the system was conducted intermittently during the period of March - August 2017.
It is confirmed through the review of relevant documents and the interview with the PPs that the monitoring activity has been appropriately implemented during the monitoring period, in line with the monitoring plan of the registered PDD.

<Findings>
Please state if CARs, CLs, or FARs are raised, and how they are resolved.
No issue was identified.

<Conclusion based on reporting requirements>
Please state conclusion based on reporting requirements.
JQA concludes that the project has been implemented in accordance with the registered PDD during the monitoring period, and no changes are found from the description of the registered PDD.

C.3. Compliance of calibration frequency and correction of measured values with related requirements

<Means of verification>
The measuring equipment used in the project activity is weight bridge (Toledo Model

JCM_ID_F_Vrf_Rep_ver01.1

IND331 Digital Indicator) made by Mettler and electricity meter (PowerLogic™ PM5300) made by Schneider Electric.

The weight bridge is calibrated yearly by Government of Karawang, Industrial and Trade Service, Regional Technical Implementation Unit for Metrology Legal, in compliance with international recommendation OIML R 76-1:2002.   The additional calibration of electricity meter is not required according to the manufacturer's specification, as described in the MPS.

It is confirmed through the review of calibration certificates that the weight bridge has been calibrated annually during the monitoring period, in accordance with the international recommendation.   Electricity meter does not require additional calibration after installation as specified by the manufacturer's specification.

Regarding the calibration of weight bridge, JQA raised CL 04 and this issue was resolved as explained in "Findings".

<Findings>
Please state if CARs, CLs, or FARs are raised, and how they are resolved.
< CL 04 >
The PP is requested to provide the calibration certificate of weight bridge during the monitoring period.

< Resolution of CL 04 by the PPs >
The calibration certificates of the weight bridge on 22/08/2017, 04/11/2017 and 27/11/2018 were provided by the PPs.   It is confirmed through the review of the calibration certificates that the first calibration of the weight bridge was delayed and conducted by UPTD Metrologi Legal under Industry, Trade, Mining and Energy Agency of Karawang District Government on 22/08/2017 after the operation of OCC Line 8 since 01/07/ 2017. As the error of the weight bridge stayed within ±5% in the result of the first calibration, the measured values of the paper production weight during the period of 01/07/2017 - 21/08/2017 were applied without correction in the calculation of emission reductions, according to the paragraph 40 (a) of JCM Guidelines for Developing Project Design Document and Monitoring Report (JCM_ID_GL_PDD_MR_ver03.0).   Thus, CL 04 is closed.

<Conclusion based on reporting requirements>
Please state conclusion based on reporting requirements.
JQA concludes that the weight bridge has been calibrated annually after the first calibration by a qualified entity and its calibration frequency is in compliance with the

> international recommendation OIML R 76-1:2002. No correction of the measured values during the period of 01/07/2017 – 21/08/2017 is required for the delayed calibration.

C.4. Assessment of data and calculation of GHG emission reductions

\<Means of verification\>

JQA has assessed the data and calculation of GHG emission reductions achieved by the project activity as follows:

(a) The corresponding Monitoring Report Sheet of the applied methodology has been used;

Through the review of the monitoring report for the project which is titled as JCM_ ID011_MP-rev4 211218.xlsx, it is confirmed that the Monitoring Report Sheets (MRS(input) 2017(7-12), MRS(calc_process) 2017(7-12), MRS(input) 2018(1-8) and MRS(calc_process) 2018(1-8)) of applied methodology ID_AM012 are appropriately used.

(b) A complete set of data for the monitoring period for all parameters monitored ex post was provided to the verification team in the form of several kinds of files.

Monitoring Report Sheet (MRS) provided by the PPs contains a complete set of the monitored data on paper production weight and electricity consumption during the monitoring period of 01/07/2017 - 31/08/2018. These data are separately provided for each year of 2017 and 2018. It is confirmed through the review of these monitored data that the paper production weight and electricity consumption are fully provided for the monitoring period.

(c) Information provided in the monitoring report has been checked with sources such as plant logbooks, inventories, purchase records, laboratory analysis;

JQA has reviewed the correctness of monitored data given in the MRS for paper production weight and electricity consumption through cross-checking them with the monthly data provided by the PPs.

Parameters	Monitored values	Method to check values in the monitoring report with sources
$PP_{j,p}$	109,777.0 (2017) 172,090.0 (2018)	The value of paper production weight in the MRS is cross-checked with monthly data which aggregates the daily data downloaded from the server.
$EC_{PJ,j,p}$	11,914.2 (2017)	The value of electricity consumption in the MRS is cross-checked with monthly data downloaded from the

JCM_ID_F_Vrf_Rep_ver01.1

	16,775.8 (2018)	server.

It is confirmed through the cross-check of the monitored data in the MRS with the monthly data that the values of paper production weight and electricity consumption in the MRS are fully consistent with the sum of their monthly data, and reference emissions ($RE_{j,p}$), project emissions ($PE_{j,p}$) and emission reductions ($ER_{j,p}$) in the MRS are correctly calculated.

(d) Any assumptions used in emission calculations have been justified;

Through the review of the MRS and the interview with the PPs, it is confirmed that no assumption has been used in the calculations of emission reductions and hence no justification is required.

(e) Appropriate emission factors, default values, and other reference values have been correctly applied.

Through the review of the MRS and the interview with the PPs, it is confirmed that CO_2 emission factor for consumed electricity (EF_{elec}) and reference specific electricity consumption of the OCC line (SEC_{RE}), which were determined at the time of validation and provided in the MPS, have been correctly applied in the calculation of reference emissions.

The data monitored and required for verification and issuance is to be kept and archived electronically for two years after the final issuance of credits.

Regarding the description in Table 1 of MRS and the difference in the emission reductions between the ex-ante and ex-post values, JQA raised CL 01 and CL 02 and these issues were resolved as explained in "Findings".

<Findings>
Please state if CARs, CLs, or FARs are raised, and how they are resolved.
< CL 01 >
Following description in Table 1 of MRS is not appropriate:
1) "The estimated value below is annual one" in (i) Monitoring frequency of Table 1 for $PP_{j,p}$ and $EC_{PJ,j,p}$,
2) "In case a calibration certificate issued by an entity accredited under national/ international standards is not provided, such measuring equipment is required to be calibrated" in (h) Measurement methods and procedures of Table 1 for $EC_{PJ,j,p}$, because electricity meter does not require additional calibration as specified in the specs in "(j) Other comments".

10

JCM_ID_F_Vrf_Rep_ver01.1

< Resolution of CL 01 by the PPs >

The PPs has submitted the revised MRS so as to keep consistency.   It is confirmed through the review of the revised MRS that the MRS is appropriately revised.   Thus, CL 01 is closed.

< CL 02 >

The PP is requested to explain the difference in the emission reductions between the ex-ante and ex-post values.

< Resolution of CL 02 by the PPs >

Following information is provided by the PPs:

The difference between real/dynamic market and expectation at the time of PDD development caused the difference of the *ex-ante* and *ex-post* values.   The largest contribution comes from the shift to the production of lighter papers driven by Chinese market.   It is confirmed through the relevant document and the interview with the PPs that PT. Fajar Surya Wisesa Tbk. produces three kinds of corrugating medium paper and the higher density paper with a basic weight of 123-127 g/m^2 is made by the OCC Line 5 which was used for the calculation of the reference specific electricity consumption of the OCC Line 5 (SEC_{RE}) at the time of the validation.   Due to the recent change of market circumstances, mainly driven by Chinese market, the demand on the lighter papers with a basic weight of 93-97 g/m^2 is increased.   This change led to the reduction of paper production weight and electricity consumption compared to their *ex-ante* estimates and accordingly caused the lower emission reductions by about 20% than the *ex-ante* value.   Thus, CL 02 is closed.

<Conclusion based on reporting requirements>

Please state conclusion based on reporting requirements.

JQA concludes that the monitored data and the project-specific parameters fixed *ex-ante* are appropriately and correctly applied in the calculation of GHG emission reductions achieved by the project activity, in accordance with the applied methodology ID_AM012 and the monitoring plan of the registered PDD.

C.5. Assessment of avoidance of double registration

<Means of verification>

It is confirmed that a written confirmation from the PPs regarding no registration under other international climate mitigation mechanisms was provided at the time of validation and the declaration letter signed by the PP's representative in the MoC was submitted to the Joint Committee.   In addition, it is re-confirmed through the check of the relevant website and the

11

JCM_ID_F_Vrf_Rep_ver01.1

interview with PPs that the project has not been registered under any other mechanisms at the time of verification.

\<Findings\>

Please state if CARs, CLs, or FARs are raised, and how they are resolved.

No issues was identified.

\<Conclusion based on reporting requirements\>

Please state conclusion based on reporting requirements.

JQA concludes that the project has not been registered under other international climate mitigation mechanisms.

C.6. Post registration changes

\<Means of verification\>

It is confirmed through the review of documents and the on-site assessment that the project has not been changed from the registered PDD and/or methodology.

\<Findings\>

Please state if CARs, CLs, or FARs are raised, and how they are resolved.

No issue was identified.

\<Conclusion based on reporting requirements\>

Please state conclusion based on reporting requirements.

JQA concludes that the project has not been changed from the registered PDD and/or methodology.

D. Assessment of response to remaining issues

An assessment of response to the remaining issues including FARs from the validation and/or previous verification period, if appropriate

No issues including FAR from the validation are remained. As this is the first verification, no issues from the previous verification are also remained.

JCM_ID_F_Vrf_Rep_ver01.1

E. Verified amount of emission reductions achieved

Year	Verified Reference Emissions (tCO₂e)	Verified Project Emissions (tCO₂e)	Verified Emission Reductions (tCO₂e)
2013	-	-	-
2014	-	-	-
2015	-	-	-
2016	-	-	-
2017	13,742.5	7,934.8	5,807
2018	21,543.2	11,172.7	10,370
2019	-	-	-
2020	-	-	-
Total (tCO₂e)			16,177

Note: The verified emission reductions in each year are rounded down after the decimal point.

F. List of interviewees and documents received

F.1. List of interviewees

- Mr. Wimba Wibawa Wanadiardja	Director, PT. Fajar Surya Wisesa Tbk.
- Mr. Marco Hardy	Finance Manager, PT. Fajar Surya Wisesa Tbk.
- Mr. Shandy Koeswanto	Corporate Finance, PT. Fajar Surya Wisesa Tbk.
- Ms. Marsha	Finance, PT. Fajar Surya Wisesa Tbk.
- Mr. Muhammad Taufiq	Head, Electrical & Instrument Department, PT. Fajar Surya Wisesa Tbk.
- Mr. Naoki Matsuo	Senior Fellow, Institute for Global Environmental Strategies (IGES)

F.2. List of documents received

1. JCM Project Design Document (ID011) _ver1.2, 27/11/2017
2. JCM Validation Report (ID011), 29/11/2017
3. Monitoring Spreadsheet: JCM_ID011_MP-rev4 211218.xlsx (Monitoring period: 01/07/2017 - 31/08/2018)
4. JCM Modalities of Communication Statement Form (ID011) (JCM_ID_F_MoC_ver01.0)
5. JCM Approved Methodology JCM_ID_AM012_ver1.0
6. JCM Glossary of Terms (JCM_ID_Glossary_ver02.0)
7. JCM Project Cycle Procedure (JCM_ID_PCP_ver05.0)

JCM_ID_F_Vrf_Rep_ver01.1

8. JCM Guidelines for Developing Project Design Document and Monitoring Report (JCM_ID_GL_PDD_MR_ver03.0)

9. JCM Guidelines for Validation and Verification (JCM_ID_GL_VV_ver01.0)

10. JCM Verification Report Form (JCM_ID_F_Vrf_Rep_ver01.1)

11. Monthly data report of electricity consumption for OCC Line 8 during the monitoring period (01/07/2017 - 31/08/2018)

12. Monthly data report of paper production weight by PM Line during the monitoring period (01/07/2017 - 31/08/2018)

13. Daily data of paper production weight during the monitoring period

14. Project specific energy consumption of OCC Line 8 during the monitoring period (Criterion 1)

15. Paper yield of the project OCC Line 8 during the monitoring period (Criterion 2)

16. Project production capacity of the OCC Line 8 during the monitoring period (Criterion 3)

17-1. Maintenance records of the OCC Line 8 (Criterion 4)

17-2. Workflow Procedure for Preventive Maintenance

18. Checklist for inspection and maintenance of OCC Line 8

19. Records and materials of operational staff training including attendee list

20. Schematic diagram of monitoring structure including information/ data flow for project activity

21. Specification of electricity meter installed at the monitoring point 2

22. Specification of weight bridge installed at the monitoring point 1

23. International Recommendation OIML R 76-1:2006, Part 1- Metrological and technical requirements – Tests

24. Calibration certificate of weight bridge dated 22/08/2017, 04/11/2017 and 27/11/2018

25. Specification of corrugating medium paper produced by PT. Fajar Surya Wisesa Tbk.

JCM_ID_F_Vrf_Rep_ver01.1

Annex Certificates or curricula vitae of TPE's verification team members, technical experts and internal technical reviewers

Please attach certificates or curricula vitae of TPE's validation team members, technical experts and internal technical reviewers.

Statement of competence   JQA

Name: Dr. Tadashi Yoshida

Qualified and authorized by Japan Quality Assurance Organization.

Function

	Date of qualification
Validator	2014/12/22
Verifier	2014/12/22
Team leader	2014/12/22

Technical area within sectoral scopes

	Date of qualification
TA 1.1. Thermal energy generation	2014/12/22
TA 1.2. Renewables	2014/12/22
TA 3.1. Energy demand	2014/12/22
TA 4.1. Cement and lime production	2015/11/12
TA 4.6. Other manufacturing industries	2014/12/22
TA 5.1. Chemical industry	2014/12/22
TA 10.1. Fugitive emissions from oil and gas	2014/12/22
TA 13.1. Solid waste and wastewater	2014/12/22
TA 14.1. Afforestation and reforestation	-

Statement of competence   JQA

Name: Mr. Hiroshi Motokawa

Qualified and authorized by Japan Quality Assurance Organization.

Function

	Date of qualification
Validator	2014/12/22
Verifier	2014/12/22
Team leader	2014/12/22

Technical area within sectoral scopes

	Date of qualification
TA 1.1. Thermal energy generation	2014/12/22
TA 1.2. Renewables	2014/12/22
TA 3.1. Energy demand	2014/12/22
TA 4.1. Cement and lime production	2014/12/22
TA 4.6. Other manufacturing industries	2014/12/22
TA 5.1. Chemical industry	-
TA 10.1. Fugitive emissions from oil and gas	-
TA 13.1. Solid waste and wastewater	2014/12/22
TA 14.1. Afforestation and reforestation	-

15

References

ADB. 2019. *Article 6 of the Paris Agreement: Drawing Lessons from the Joint Crediting Mechanism.* Manila.

———. 2020. *Decoding Article 6 of the Paris Agreement Version II.* Manila.

Bodansky, D. 2016. The Legal Character of the Paris Agreement. *Review of European, Comparative, and International Environmental Law, Forthcoming.* 22 March.

Boer, R. et al. 2018. Indonesia Second Biennial Update Report under the United Nations Framework Convention on Climate Change. Jakarta: Directorate General of Climate Change, Ministry of Environment and Forestry.

Conference of the Parties Serving as the Meeting of the Parties to the Paris Agreement. 2021. *Nationally Determined Contributions under the Paris Agreement–Synthesis Report by the Secretariat,* FCCC/PA/CMA/2021/2 (26 February).

Conference of the Parties Serving as the Meeting of the Parties to the Paris Agreement. 2019. *Report of the Conference of the Parties Serving as the Meeting of the Parties to the Paris Agreement on the Third Part of its First Session, Held in Katowice from 2 to 15 December 2018–Addendum–Part Two: Action Taken by the Conference of the Parties Serving as the Meeting of the Parties to the Paris Agreement,* FCCC/PA/CMA/2018/3/Add.2 (19 March).

Development Asia. 2019. Advanced Battery Technology to Integrate Intermittent Renewables in the Maldives.

Government of Indonesia. 2021. *Updated Nationally Determined Contribution.* Jakarta.

Government of Japan. 2021. *Recent Developments of The Joint Crediting Mechanism (JCM).* July.

Joint Crediting Mechanism. 2015. *Joint Crediting Mechanism Rules of Procedures for the Joint Committee.*

———. 2018. *Joint Crediting Mechanism Guidelines for Developing Proposed Methodology.*

JCM Indonesia Secretariat. 2017. ID_AM012 - Reduction of Energy Consumption by Introducing an Energy-Efficient Old Corrugated Carton Processing System into a Cardboard Factory.

———. ID011 Reduction of Energy Consumption by Introducing an Energy-Efficient Waste Paper Processing System into a Packaging Paper Factory in Bekasi, West Java.

———. Issuance of Credits (accessed 19 September 2021).

———. Joint Committee.

———. *Joint Crediting Mechanism Guidelines for Developing Sustainable Development Implementation Plan and Report.*

————. *Kerjasama Bilateral tentang Joint Crediting Mechanism untuk Kemitraan Pertumbuhan Rendah Karbon antara Republik Indonesia dan Jepang.*

————. Registered Projects.

————. Third Party Entities.

Ministry of the Environment of Japan. The Joint Crediting Mechanism Registry System.

Michaelowa, A. et al. 2019. Additionality Revisited: Guarding the Integrity of Market Mechanisms under the Paris Agreement. *Climate Policy.* 19 (10). pp. 1211–1224.

Murun, T. and A. Tsukui. 2020. *Joint Crediting Mechanism Contributions to Sustainable Development Goals.* Tokyo: Ministry of the Environment, Government of Japan.

National Registry System on Climate Change Control.

————. List of Emission Reduction Actions (accessed 24 September 2021).

Schneider, L., A. Kollmuss, and M. Lazarus. 2014. Addressing the Risk of Double Counting Emission Reductions under the UNFCCC. *Stockholm Environment Institute Working Papers.* No. 2014-02. Stockholm: Stockholm Environment Institute.

Spalding-Fecher, R. et al. 2020. *Practical Strategies to Avoid Over-selling—Final Report.*

UNEP DTU Partnership, Centre on Energy, Climate and Sustainable Development. UNEP DTU Article 6 Pipeline Analysis and Database (accessed 19 September 2021).

UNFCCC. Global Warming Potentials (IPCC Fourth Assessment Report).

————. Draft Text on Matters relating to Article 6 of the Paris Agreement: Guidance on Cooperative Approaches Referred to in Article 6, Paragraph 2, of the Paris Agreement. Version 3. 15 December 2019.

www.ingramcontent.com/pod-product-compliance
Lightning Source LLC
Chambersburg PA
CBHW061220270326
41926CB00032B/4792